Five-Minute Crimebusters
Clever Mini-Mysteries

Stan Smith
Illustrated by Kathleen O'Malley

Sterling Publishing Co., Inc.
New York

To Julie and Jennifer

"Crime is common. Logic is rare. Therefore it is upon the logic, rather than upon the crime, that you should dwell."

—Sherlock Holmes

Library of Congress Cataloging-in-Publication Data Available

20 19 18 17 16

Published by Sterling Publishing Co., Inc.
387 Park Avenue South, New York, NY 10016
© 2000 by Stanley Smith
Distributed in Canada by Sterling Publishing
c/o Canadian Manda Group, 165 Dufferin Street,
Toronto, Ontario, Canada M6K 3H6
Distributed in Great Britain and Europe by Chris Lloyd at Orca Book
Services, Stanley House, Fleets Lane, Poole BH15 3AJ, England
Distributed in Australia by Capricorn Link (Australia) Pty. Ltd.
P.O. Box 704, Windsor, NSW 2756, Australia

Sterling ISBN 0-8069-1827-6

For information about custom editions, special sales, premium and
corporate purchases, please contact Sterling Special Sales
Department at 800-805-5489 or specialsales@sterlingpub.com.

CONTENTS

Introduction 5

The Stockbroker's Last Morning .7

A Model Murder 10

The Adventure of the Negative Clue 13

A New Year's Dissolution 17

The Case of the Invisible Murderer 20

Death Brings Down the Curtain 24

Death of a Kingpin 27

A Death by the Thames 30

The Table of Death 32

Murder at Big Jake's 34

Murder by the Wayward 36

Death at the Clinic 38

The Stolen War Club Caper 40

The Case of the Royston Reindeer 43

Memorial Day Mischief 46

The Phony Faith Healer 49

Sabotage at Centipore 51

The Bracken Park Incident 54

The Case of the Bulgarian Diamonds 56

The Case of the Bulgonian Spy 58

One Morning at the Festival 60

Chief Ryan Pays a Call 62

The Powers' Predicament 64

An Idyll Day in Edinburgh 66

Room at the Inn 68

The Prom Date Puzzle 70

Stanwick Solves a Pie Puzzle .72

Stanwick at Chartwell 74

The Tale of the Generous Rajah 76

The Case of the Contentious Cows 80

Babies for the Bulletin 82

Stanwick at the Circus 84

Solutions 86

Index 96

CONTENTS

Introduction 5

The Stockbroker's Last Morning 7

A Model Murder 10

The Adventure of the Negative Clue 13

A New Year's Dissolution 17

The Case of the Invisible Murderer 20

Death Brings Down the Curtain 24

Death of a Kingpin 27

A Death by the Thames 30

The Table of Death 32

Murder at Big Jake's 34

Murder by the Wayward 36

Death at the Clinic 38

The Stolen War Club Caper 40

The Case of the Royston Reindeer 43

Memorial Day Mischief 46

The Phony Faith Healer 49

Sabotage at Centipore 51

The Bracken Park Incident 54

The Case of the Bulgarian Diamonds 56

The Case of the Bulgonian Spy 58

One Morning at the Festival 60

Chief Ryan Pays a Call 62

The Powers' Predicament 64

An Idyll Day in Edinburgh 66

Room at the Inn 68

The Prom Date Puzzle 70

Stanwick Solves a Pie Puzzle 72

Stanwick at Chartwell 74

The Tale of the Generous Rajah 76

The Case of the Contentious Cows 80

Babies for the Bulletin 82

Stanwick at the Circus 84

Solutions 86

Index 96

Introduction

WELCOME BACK, sleuths and solvers, to the puzzling world of amateur logician Thomas P. Stanwick! Some of his earlier adventures in logic have been chronicled in *Five-Minute Whodunits*. From his home in the small town of Baskerville and in his travels in New England and the British Isles, Stanwick uses his amazing powers of deduction to help the police and others solve many a baffling crime. He also helps friends and neighbors in Baskerville solve less felonious, but equally puzzling, mysteries of their own.

Stanwick helps Inspector Matt Walker of the Royston Police, Inspector Gilbert Bodwin of Scotland Yard, and attorney Amanda Tucker solve murders in Royston, London, and elsewhere. Sometimes Stanwick visits the scene, but at other times

he deduces the solution from the comfort of an armchair. His cases include robbery, fraud, espionage, and general high jinks at home and abroad. And sometimes Stanwick helps a friend or a neighbor logically untie a puzzling problem.

These cases require Thomas Stanwick to deduce essential facts from physical circumstances, separate liars from truthtellers, infer who has what role in a gang or crime, and reason with elementary mathematics or time sequences. So get ready to test and sharpen your logical thinking skills and help Stanwick unravel these brand-new mystery puzzles!

The Stockbroker's Last Morning

SHORTLY AFTER NINE one morning, Inspector Walker's car pulled up in front of a large office building in downtown Royston. With Walker was Thomas P. Stanwick, the amateur logician. Stanwick had been visiting Walker at headquarters when the call reporting the sudden death of Charles Steinberg had come in.

Stanwick and Walker hurried to Steinberg's seventh-floor office suite, from which he had run a prosperous stock brokerage firm. Passing through the carpeted reception area, they entered Steinberg's spacious office.

Steinberg's body was slumped in an easy chair near a small, circular table in the center of the room. His tie and collar were loose. He had been dead for less than an hour, and showed no sign of bleeding. On a small table by the wall, a typewriter contained a typed note, which Stanwick read aloud.

> I see no further purpose to my life and have therefore decided to end it. I hope my family, friends, and associates will not blame themselves.
>
> Goodbye.

Walker turned to the man in his early 30's who was standing near the office door. Jon Golding was a vice president of the firm.

"What can you tell us, Mr. Golding?"

Golding coughed nervously.

"I entered Mr. Steinberg's office earlier this morning to see him on urgent business. He was sitting in the easy chair with a cup of coffee in his hand. As soon as he saw me, he hastily drank it down. The cup had no sooner left his lips than he was seized with terrible convulsions. A few seconds later he was dead. I was horrified and ran out to the receptionist's desk, where I phoned for help. No one was allowed into the office until you arrived."

"Did you see the note in the typewriter?"

"No, sir, I did not."

"Thank you." Walker went over to Steinberg's body and searched his pockets. In the right jacket pocket he found a small glass vial, which he sniffed. "This probably contained the poison."

Stanwick sniffed it and, taking out his handkerchief, picked up the emptied coffee cup from its saucer on the table and sniffed it also.

"I can detect a whiff of it here, too," he said.

Stanwick put down the coffee cup and faced Golding.

"Mr. Golding," he asked, "did Mr. Steinberg usually have his coffee in that chair?"

"Yes, sir, he drank his coffee and read the paper in that chair every morning about this time."

Stanwick pointed to a newspaper folded neatly on the table. "Did you put that there?"

Golding flushed slightly. "It was there when I came in. He wasn't reading it."

Stanwick abruptly left the office and walked to the desk of the young receptionist.

"What can you tell us, Miss Gwynne?"

"Why, little enough, I'm afraid. I heard some typing in Mr. Steinberg's office, and then Mr. Golding came out of his own office to pick up some documents for Mr. Steinberg. He went into Mr. Steinberg's office and a few moments later came rushing wildly out here and phoned for help."

"What documents did he want to show Mr. Steinberg?"

"Why, some draft pages of our weekly newsletter. He dropped them on the floor as he came back out."

Reentering Steinberg's office, Stanwick put another question to Golding. "I see there is a door between your office and this. Why didn't you use that when you came in to see him?"

"Miss Gwynne, our receptionist, had the newsletter pages I wanted to show him," Golding answered.

Stanwick quietly drew Walker aside.

"Golding is lying, Matt," he said. "This isn't suicide, but murder!"

How does Stanwick know Golding is lying?

Solution on page 89.

9

A Model Murder

CURIOSITY AND SADNESS mingled in the mind of Thomas P. Stanwick, the amateur logician, as he parked his car near the home of Lola Monteray in Royston. His friend Inspector Matt Walker had called to tell him of the murder of the beautiful young model and had invited him to have a look at the scene. Not even the intellectual satisfaction of studying crimes could blot out for Stanwick the tragedy of untimely death.

He entered the trim, white Monteray home and was shown upstairs. Walker was in the bedroom. The body of Lola Monteray, in a lacy nightgown, lay prone on the blood-soaked bedsheets. A large, blood-covered knife lay beside the bed.

"The coroner estimates that Lola Monteray was stabbed to death around two o'clock last night," said Walker briskly. "No prints in here except hers. She was discovered this morning by Thomas Larch, her agent, who says he stopped by to take her to an important meeting with some designers. He found the back door unlocked and searched the house until he found her here."

Stanwick glanced around the plainly furnished room and toyed with the tip of his mustache.

"Have you found a possible motive?" he asked.

Walker shook his head.

"Not yet. She seems to have been successful and well liked. Her appointment book shows that she had lunch with her boyfriend, Scott Phillips, two days ago. I called him and told him she had been found dead at her home. He said he'd come right over. When he arrives, he might be able to tell us if anything unusual was going on in her life."

The two men left the room and went downstairs. A pudgy man with a dark Lincoln beard sat in the living room, looking crushed with grief.

"Mr. Larch, I presume," said Stanwick with a nod as he strode

in. "I understand that you found the body."

"Yes," the agent replied, his head bowed. "An awful sight!"

"Why were you so persistent as to enter and search the house to find her?"

Larch looked up wearily. "We had a 10:30 appointment at the Picardio Studio," he said. "This was an important meeting that might have led to a lucrative contract, and she knew it. I wasn't going to lose a deal like that so that she could sleep late!"

At that moment the front door was flung open with a crash, and a disheveled young man ran up the stairs.

"Who stabbed my sweetheart?" he shouted. "Let me see her!"

A policeman stopped him at the top of the stairs and brought him forcibly down to the living room.

"Mr. Phillips?" said Walker. "I'm very sorry. The crime scene is accessible only to investigators. Miss Monteray was killed about two last night and was discovered this morning. Her appointment book shows that you two had lunch together on Tuesday. Did she give any indication that someone was threatening her?"

Phillips thrust his hands into his pockets and paced the rug.

"No, nothing. She was excited about an appointment to visit Picardio's this morning, and talked about the work she hoped to do for them. She was very happy."

Stanwick, ensconced in an armchair, watched idly as Phillips paced.

"Where did you eat?" he asked.

"Marygold's, downtown," answered Phillips. "She loved their asparagus tips."

"The best in town." Stanwick arose languidly and stretched. "Well, Matt, earn your pay. It's time to arrest the killer!"

Who murdered Lola Monteray?

Solution on page 86.

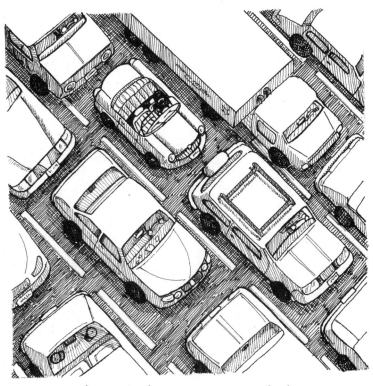

The Adventure of the
Negative Clue

NOT EVEN THE UNUSUAL heat of that late spring day could dis-
suade Thomas P. Stanwick from driving into the city. The
amateur logician had learned that one of Royston's most select
book dealers was holding a sale of rare folios at two in the afternoon. His bibliophilic instincts aroused, Stanwick was braving
the heat and the downtown traffic he detested when the police
radio in his car reported a murder nearby.

A middle-aged man had been stabbed to death in Hardee's
Hardware Store three blocks away. Squad cars were told to

watch for a white male of five feet, ten inches, 160 pounds, about 22 years old, with black hair and a pencil mustache, wearing a white T-shirt, a leather jacket, and blue jeans.

Stanwick wrestled with his competing interests for two seconds and then turned toward the hardware store. Parking his car down the block, he walked through a curious throng and, with a flash of his police pass, entered the shop. Inspector Walker arched his sandy eyebrows in surprise as he caught sight of his friend.

"Hello, Matt," said Stanwick. "I heard the bulletin on the radio and thought I'd stop by for a look."

"Glad to see you, Tom." Walker nodded to a dead body crumpled on the floor in front of the sales counter. "There's what there is to look at."

The victim was a dark-haired man in his middle 40's. He lay faceup. The handle of a knife protruded from his ribs, and a circle of blood had soaked through his blue suit.

"His wallet is missing," Walker reported drily, "as is a briefcase the sales clerk said he was carrying when he came in. From other papers in his pockets, we've identified him as Hubert French, an accounting executive from Helston."

"Did the clerk see it happen?" asked Stanwick, glancing at a thin, balding man lurking behind the counter.

"No. He says French came in to pick up a special wrench he had ordered. A guy fitting the bulletin description came in just a few seconds later. The clerk went to the back to get the wrench. While there, he heard sounds of a scuffle and a cry from here. He rushed in and found French dead and the other fellow gone."

Stanwick fingered the tip of his mustache. "Any prints on the weapon?"

Walker shook his head. "No. The clerk says our suspect wore gloves."

Just then the outer door opened, and two policemen entered with a manacled man closely fitting the description given on the radio.

"Inspector, this is T. A. Orrison," said the older officer. "We found him four blocks away, walking briskly down Jefferson. Says he was on his way home after slicing fish in the back of Radford's Fish Mart all morning. He fits the description, though, so we picked him up."

Walker looked coldly at Orrison, who was wearing green sunglasses.

"What do you know about this, Mr. Orrison?" he demanded, pointing at the corpse.

"Nothing," Orrison replied angrily. "I was at work all morning. I haven't been in this place for at least three weeks."

"How long have you worked at Radford's?"

"Two months now, part-time. I work from seven to noon, six days a week. I put in some overtime today and was just on the way home when I was grabbed by these two guys in a squad car and brought here."

A mild, metallic odor suffused the small shop. Stanwick wandered to a window, opened it partway, and gazed idly out. Walker continued his questions.

"You implied that you visited this shop a few weeks ago. Why?"

"I dunno. I had to get nails or tape or something."

"Why did you work late today?"

"We got a big catch in this morning, and I was the only one there."

Walker signaled to the uniformed officers. "All right, that's enough for here. Take him to the station for more questioning."

Once the others had left, Stanwick rejoined the inspector.

"When you get back, Matt," he said, "you may as well book him for the murder. He's your man."

Walker turned to him in astonishment. "What makes you so sure? I'll admit he's on shaky ground, but I don't see any conclusive clue."

Stanwick smiled.

"In a way, there isn't one," he replied. "What's really significant in this case is what you could call a negative clue—the one that isn't here!"

What is the negative clue?

Solution on page 94.

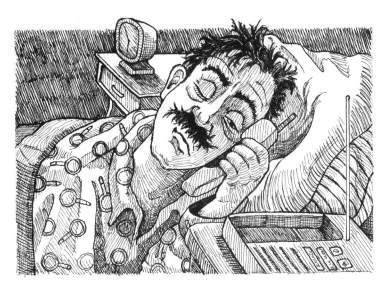

A New Year's Dissolution

THOMAS P. STANWICK was still fighting off sleep as he mounted the front steps of the Dunhope home in Royston. Some way to begin a new year, he thought. After attending a New Year's Eve party, the amateur logician had been roused at six by a phone call from Inspector Walker. Robert Dunhope of Dunhope & Henson, a prosperous insurance agency, had been poisoned at a New Year's Eve party in his home, and Walker had asked Stanwick to have a look.

"Happy New Year, Tom," said Walker dourly at the door. "This way."

Walker led Stanwick into a large, well-furnished living room. Three men and a woman, still in evening clothes, sat numbly on a long sofa.

"The body has been removed," said Walker. "Mrs. Dunhope has gone down to headquarters."

"These four, I take it, were the guests at the party?" said Stanwick.

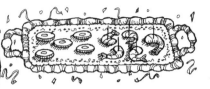

"That's right. John Meridale is—was—Dunhope's accountant. Harriet Schultze is a friend of Mrs. Dunhope and has written several popular cookbooks. Simon Henson is the junior partner in Dunhope's firm, and George Dunhope is the victim's nephew."

Stanwick sat down in an armchair across from the sofa and glanced quickly around the room. Walker took out his official notebook.

"I'd like to ask the four of you to repeat to Mr. Stanwick what you remember about the events of last night," said the inspector.

Henson, a haggard man with a trim, dark beard, gave a long sigh.

"Up until midnight," he said, "it was pretty much the same party we have together every New Year's Eve, except for George being with us."

"I'm starting my graduate studies at Royston State next week," said George. "I've been staying with Aunt Grace and Uncle Bob until I can find a place of my own in the city."

"What went on until midnight?" asked Stanwick.

"Oh, you know," said Miss Schultze, "punch, eggnog, conversation. Bob and John started a game of chess. Shortly before midnight, Simon and I passed out some hors d'oeuvres I had prepared." She clenched a crumpled cocktail napkin and brushed away a tear.

Stanwick began toying with the tip of his mustache.

"And what happened at midnight?" he asked.

"As the hour approached," said Meridale, "we all stood up, and I filled everyone's glass with Champagne. When midnight struck, we all cheered 'Happy New Year' and drank a toast. In doing so, Simon accidentally bumped into Bob and caused him to spill some of his Champagne, but it was quickly cleaned up.

"A few moments later, though, Bob just collapsed. We thought it was a heart attack and called an ambulance. By the time the medics arrived, Bob was already dead. They checked him, said it looked suspicious, and called in the police."

"Thank you. Excuse us a moment." Stanwick stood up and stepped into the hallway with Walker. "What has the medical examiner found, Matt?"

Walker grimaced and scratched the back of his neck.

"Doc Pillsbury says it looks like a fast-acting poison. We've tested the Champagne remaining in Dunhope's glass and stained on his clothing, though, and there's no trace of poison."

"How about the hors d'oeuvres?"

"The guests say he ate only half of one. The half he didn't eat checked out clean. He didn't eat or drink anything else."

"Any food or strange objects in his pockets?"

"No, just keys, change, and a comb. That's what has us stumped, Tom. He must have been poisoned right around midnight, but we can't even figure out how he ingested the stuff."

Stanwick gave a gaping yawn before replying.

"Excuse me," he said. "If Pillsbury's results are confirmed, and no more significant facts come to light, I think I can point out the method of murder and the likely murderer."

Who murdered Dunhope, and how?

Solution on page 87.

The Case
of the
Invisible
Murderer

THOMAS P. STANWICK, the amateur logician, and Inspector
Matthew Walker of the Royston Police Department were
grateful for the sea breeze on that hot August day as they walked
from Walker's car to the entryway of the Sea Maiden restaurant.
The two had been discussing another case in Walker's office
when the call had come in about a murder at the Sea Maiden.

Inside the stuffy restaurant, two uniformed officers were
recording the names and addresses of those who had been there
when the body was discovered. The discovery had occurred at
3:30, less than an hour before Stanwick and Walker arrived, so
only six patrons—one couple and a family of four—were being
detained. They sat in a row of chairs along a side wall. With
them were a cashier, a busboy, two waiters, two waitresses, and
the chef.

Walker introduced himself to the agitated owner of the restaurant, Steven Evans. Evans, Walker, and Stanwick then passed through the main dining room, which contained 17 tables, to a smaller dining room on the right.

"Hello, Ernie," said Walker to the police photographer. "Are you fellows about through?"

"Just about. Jim is still dusting for prints."

The smaller room was connected to the main room by an open doorway. One of the five tables still had dirty utensils and dishes of half-eaten food. Slumped across this table was the dead man, a wealthy publishing executive named Gerald Hottleman. A knife protruded from his back.

"It was a restaurant steak knife with no prints," reported the fingerprinter. "Wiped clean." Walker nodded and glanced around the plainly decorated room. Several small windows near the ceiling did little to relieve the warmth and stuffiness of the room. An odor of fish lingered in the air.

"How was the body discovered?" Walker asked Evans.

"About an hour ago, Kris, the waitress for this room, started to come in to ask Mr. Hottleman if he wanted coffee or dessert," replied the perspiring owner. "She saw him from the doorway and stood there, screaming."

"No one else was in this room, then?" asked Stanwick.

"He was the only one in here. An elderly couple who had lunch here left about 20 minutes before we found Mr. Hottleman."

"Did anyone see Hottleman alive after they left?" Walker inquired.

"Oh, yes. When the old folks were about halfway to the cash register, Mr. Hottleman came out and gave the lady her sunglasses, which she had left on the table."

"Then Hottleman came back here?"

"That's right."

"And who else entered the room between the time Hottleman returned to his table and the time his body was discovered?"

"Why, no one, Inspector. The other guests were in the main dining room, and Kris was on break."

Stanwick eyed the owner quizzically. "How can you be sure that no one slipped into this room?" he asked.

"I was sitting at a small table near the cash register looking over our receipts," Evans replied, "and I would have noticed it."

Just then the medical examiner's staff entered the room to remove the body. Evans excused himself and hurried off. Walker returned to the main room to talk to the uniformed officers. Stanwick lingered in the small room and glanced about, thoughtfully fingering a tip of his mustache.

No doorways led into the room except the one from the main dining room. The windows were too small for human entry and too high up for the knife to have been thrown in from outside, even if the angle of the knife in the body permitted such a hypothesis. Stanwick frowned, returned to the main room, and took Walker aside.

"Matt, was anything taken?" he asked quietly.

"Hottleman's wallet is gone. If you mean evidence, nothing was touched until we arrived."

"Then how was Hottleman identified?"

"The owner and staff here know him. He's been here many times."

"Rather late for lunch, isn't it?" Stanwick smiled slightly.

Walker shrugged. "Not everyone thought so."

The two walked back to the side room and paused by the doorway. Photographers, fingerprinters, and medical examiners were gone, as were the dead man and the murder weapon. The busboy apologetically brushed by Stanwick and Walker with a small cart and began to clear away the effects of the victim's table.

"We're still taking statements," said Walker quietly, "but everything we've heard so far corroborates the owner's story. He was seated at the table near the cash register the whole time. Frankly, Tom, I'm puzzled. The only way anyone could enter the

room is through this doorway. No one was in there after the old couple left except for Hottleman; he was seen re-entering the room; and no one else was seen entering the room until the body was discovered."

"An impossible crime, eh?" chuckled Stanwick. "Or at least a crime committed by an invisible killer. Well, there are more ways than one to be invisible, my friend. I can tell you who the murderer is."

Who murdered Hottleman?

Solution on page 91.

Death Brings Down the Curtain

T WO SHOTS CRACKED from the barrel of the pistol. Morton Hooper, playing the invidious Sam Spearon, crumpled to the stage floor as Lady Carneval (Vanessa Netherwood) and her niece (Elizabeth Murdoch) screamed in horror. The gun still in her hand, Lizzy Belle (Ann Doherty) then fled the stage with her admirer, Ned Hester (Ken Lynch).

The Royston Community Players production of the popular farce "Two Bullets Too Many" was off to a rollicking start. Five minutes after the gunplay, Scene 3 came to an end. Only Netherwood and Murdoch remained on the partly darkened stage during the brief scene change.

Scene 4 opened with a conversation between them. Several minutes into the scene, Lizzy Belle reappeared on stage ranting and waving the pistol. After some wild dialogue, Lizzy took sudden aim and fired two shots at Lady Carneval. This time, however, the fall to the floor and the blood were a little too lifelike, and the screams were genuine.

Thomas P. Stanwick stood up in the audience. "Curtain!"

Some two hours later, the members of the audience had given their names and addresses and had been sent home. The cast and crew were in the greenroom being questioned by the reliable Sergeant Hatch. Stanwick and Inspector Matthew Walker were standing on the otherwise deserted stage, near the bloodstain on the floor.

"It couldn't have been an accident," said Walker. "The props manager, whom I know and trust, has years of experience, and he knows blanks from real bullets. He swears he filled the gun with blanks before the show."

"I think we can rule out suicide, too," Stanwick replied. "Miss Netherwood was on stage the whole time between the shooting of Sam Spearon, which was done with blanks, and the second

shooting. She therefore had no chance to change the bullets. She would have had to use an accomplice, and that would have been too risky for both."

"I agree." Walker sighed. "So murder it was. The first shooting was at 8:40 P.M. Miss Doherty immediately left the stage, dumped the gun in the prop box, and returned to the greenroom to have her makeup touched up. At 8:55 P.M., she picked up the gun again and reappeared on stage. So the bullets must have been switched during that 15-minute interval. And backstage is not accessible to the public."

Just then Sergeant Hatch approached to report to Walker.

"I've finished the preliminary questioning, sir," he said. "The stage crew, including the props manager, were in constant communication with one another, and no one had a chance to get to the gun in the prop box during the critical interval. The director was in the audience with some friends.

"Miss Doherty and Mr. Lynch vouch for each other and went to the greenroom between scenes. The makeup artist, who was expecting them, confirms this. Miss Netherwood and Miss Murdoch remained on stage between shootings. Mr. Hooper, the first 'victim,' left the stage at the end of Scene 3, stopped to get a soda from the vending machine, and returned to the greenroom."

"Aren't two other actors in the show?" Walker asked. "Where were they?"

"Lester Sack and Jill Richart were in the greenroom the entire time, waiting to go on in Act II. The best consensus we can get is that Scene 4 opened at 8:47 P.M.; Miss Doherty reappeared with the gun at 8:55 P.M.; and Miss Netherwood was shot at 9:01 P.M."

"Thank you, Hatch. Carry on." Walker turned to Stanwick. "Apparently some more questioning is in order."

"Indeed," said Stanwick. "Especially with the prime suspect."

Who is Stanwick's prime suspect, and why?

Solution on page 89.

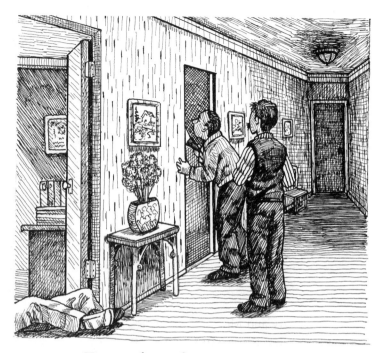

Death of a Kingpin

THOMAS P. STANWICK'S VISIT that day to Inspector Walker's office was particularly well timed. Walker was just leaving to visit the scene of the murder of Aaron Griffith of Hubbard Drive, a moneyed neighborhood, and he invited the amateur logician to join him.

"Frankly, I'm not surprised Griffith took a bullet," remarked Walker during the drive. "Two, actually. He was a drug kingpin, and we'd been watching him for some time. He worked from an upstairs office in his home with a bodyguard outside the door. Not much of a retinue for someone in his position."

"It sounds like the bodyguard had his limitations," Stanwick observed.

Walker grunted. "Well, he paid the price for them. He was

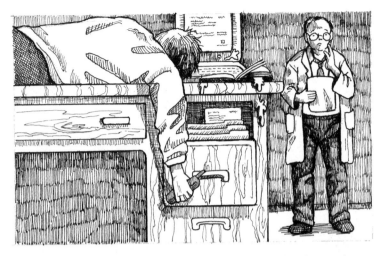

gunned down too. Griffith had enough life left after being shot to call 9-1-1. Listen to this."

Walker inserted a cassette tape into his tape deck and pressed a button. A moment later a desperate voice filled the car.

"This is Griffith...I've been shot...It was Ren...Ren...."

"Too bad he couldn't get out the rest of the name," said Walker as he stopped the tape. "His appointment book showed that he saw a delegation of three men this morning: Albert Wrenville, Barry Renfeld, and Carl Rennecker."

"Ren, Ren, and Ren," murmured Stanwick. "At least phonetically. Any other visitors that we know of?"

"Only his sister from across town. Flora. Well, here we are."

Two minutes later, Walker and Stanwick were standing by the body of the guard outside the door to Griffith's office. The door was at the end of a long hardwood hallway. Five feet down from the guard, a wall section was slid back to reveal a passage within the wall. Walker looked inside it and whistled softly.

"A hidden passage!" he exclaimed. "You don't often see one of these. But I suppose Griffith wanted an escape route." He and Stanwick stepped into the carpeted, paneled office of the victim, where Sergeant Hatch joined them.

"The guard was shot at close range, sir," he reported to

Walker. "Two to three feet. Doc Pillsbury says he was killed first. Griffith appears to have been shot from the doorway. It's about 20 feet from there to the desk."

The desk, a massive creation of oak, stood in the center of the room facing the doorway. Slumped over the desk in his own blood lay the kingpin, his right hand clutching the telephone. The still-lit computer console, the gold pen set, several folders, and the appointment diary were spattered with blood as well. At the desk and elsewhere in the room, the investigative team worked quietly and efficiently.

"Shot in the chest and the throat, to use layman's terms," Pillsbury, the medical examiner, noted tersely. "Amazed he could still talk, but it's not impossible."

"Who were the Rens, anyway?" Stanwick suddenly asked Walker.

"More dirtbags. Wrenville had drug connections in South America and had just come up from there. This was his first meeting with Griffith. Renfeld belongs to one of the big drug 'families'; he's done business with Griffith a couple of times before. Rennecker, who used to be Griffith's personal assistant, is his affiliate (so to speak) in the western part of the state. I looked them up on the police network before heading over here."

"And his sister—was she here before the Rens?"

"Yes, at 8:30. The Rens were here at 10. It looks like one of the Rens, who came in separate cars, either lingered behind or returned alone. They apparently have no common interest in Griffith's death."

"In that case, one or two at least plausible deductions can be made," said Stanwick. "For one, it was indeed one of the Rens. For another, I think I can name which one it was."

Who murdered Griffith?

Solution on page 93.

A Death by the Thames

"**P**OOR LADY MADGE!" exclaimed Judith Woolbrott. "Sir Alan done to death, her jewels taken, the silver taken—how will she bear it?" The petite maid burst into tears again.

"We have no more questions for now, young lady," said Inspector Gilbert Bodwin of Scotland Yard. "Please remain here."

The inspector and his companion, Thomas P. Stanwick, returned up the stairs to the elegant flat of Sir Alan and Lady Madge Tewksbury. The couple, a prominent industrialist and his wife, lived just across the Thames from Parliament.

"I'm sorry to take you away from your Churchill Society conference, Tom," said Bodwin, "but I thought this case would interest you. You don't often visit London in November."

"Always glad to be on hand," replied Stanwick as they entered the flat. He and the inspector passed through a small foyer into the living room. An armchair was overturned, and a mahogany case on the sideboard had been torn open and emptied.

"Sir Alan was found lying on the rug in the middle of the room," said Bodwin. "His body has been removed. The examiner's preliminary report is that he was stunned by a blow and then strangled by a pair of large and powerful hands."

Stanwick fingered the tip of his mustache. "The maid, if I recall her answers, reported for duty at 10, found the door unlocked, and then entered the living room and discovered the body. After a fit of screaming, she ran down to the neighbor's flat and has remained there since."

"That's right," said Bodwin. "She clearly is not the murderer, since her hands are much too small and weak. Sir Alan apparently surprised a burglar, who killed him and escaped with some of the family silver—there is the rifled case on the sideboard—and Lady Madge's jewels from her case in the bedroom. Her Ladyship is on her way back from a trip to Scotland."

"How much have she and Miss Woolbrott been told?" asked Stanwick.

"Her Ladyship has been told only the essentials. The maid had to be sedated, and has been told only that her Ladyship is returning."

"Excellent!" Stanwick took his pipe from his pocket, then replaced it with a sheepish grin. "Of course, no smoking at a crime scene. Anyway, I recommend that you question Miss Woolbrott further. She didn't commit the murder herself, but I think she knows who did!"

Why does Stanwick think so?

Solution on page 91.

The Table of Death

Just as Inspector Walker's hand was hovering over a bishop, his beeper alarm sounded. With an impatient sigh, he pushed back his chair and stood up. Across the chessboard, Thomas P. Stanwick chuckled softly.

"Saved by the beep!" he exclaimed.

"Don't be so sure of that!" Walker retorted as he started toward the Royston Chess Club lobby and a telephone. One minute later, he was back.

"Gotta go," he said hurriedly. "Two bodies in an apartment. Want to come?"

"Certainly."

Twenty minutes later, Stanwick and Walker were in a seedy, third-floor apartment downtown. The place consisted of a bedroom and a small kitchen off a sparsely furnished sitting room. In the center of the sitting room stood a square wooden table supporting a half-full pitcher of purple liquid, two drained glasses, several incense candles, a few small piles of powder, and a handwritten note with two signatures.

On the floor by the table lay the bodies of two middle-aged

men, each by an overturned wooden chair. Sergeant Hatch and the crime scene unit were already at work when Walker and Stanwick arrived.

"The fellow in the undershirt is George Barnes, the tenant here," Hatch reported. "The one in the suit is Theo Hunter, an insurance salesman. We've checked their pockets. The candles and drugs are similar to those used in some cult out West. The note, signed by both, is a suicide pact. It's pretty weird, sir."

"Will that word appear on your report, sergeant?" said Walker with a wry half-smile. "Let's see what was in their pockets."

"This way, sir." Hatch led them to a side table. "Barnes had these tissues and keys, and this comb and wallet. The rest is Hunter's. Handkerchief, keys, penknife, business cards, wallet, comb, a folded gas receipt from earlier today, a folded insurance application from last week."

"Hmm." Walker turned to the approaching medical examiner. "Any verdict, Doc?"

"Not yet, of course," replied Dr. Pillsbury peevishly. "You must await the autopsy. The external symptoms, though, are of a swift-acting poison."

Walker glanced at Stanwick. "You've been awfully quiet, Tom."

Stanwick, who had been leaning against the wall and staring at the table, snapped out of his reverie.

"It's a small room and a busy investigation," he said. "Just trying to stay out of the way. I suggest that you check the signatures on that note carefully, though."

"Oh?" Walker arched his sandy eyebrows. "That's routine, of course, but why do you say that?"

"I think one of the signatures is forged. This looks to me like a murder-suicide. One poisoned the other and then made it look like a double suicide. And I can tell you which was the murderer."

Which was the murderer? How does Stanwick know?

Solution on page 94.

Murder at Big Jake's

I T WAS LATE IN the afternoon of a fine spring day when Thomas P. Stanwick, the amateur logician, waved Inspector Matthew Walker into the living room of his Baskerville bungalow. Stanwick, who was recovering from the flu, was dressed in pajamas, slippers, and a dark blue robe. Rufus, his black Labrador, looked up and flopped his tail when the two men entered the room and then the dog resumed gnawing a plastic bone.

"Glad to hear you're feeling better, Tom," said Walker. He sat down and accepted a can of cold beer.

"I'm getting there, thanks," said Stanwick with a weak smile. He sat down and put his feet on an ottoman. "Haven't had the strength to do much more than read, but I'm behind on the newspapers. What's new in city crime?"

"Well, let's see." Walker took a sip of beer. "A few nights ago, at about two A.M., a drug pusher named Valenzi was shot and killed on the sidewalk in front of Big Jake's bar. A drifter named Albert Gummond was arrested near the scene.

"Although no one saw the actual shooting, witnesses in the

bar have identified Gummond as having quarreled with Valenzi there shortly beforehand. Not about drugs, though—about a woman. Gummond left the bar immediately after Valenzi. The gun hasn't been found yet, but Gummond had blood on his jacket when he was picked up. The blood is being tested."

Stanwick lit his pipe. "Has Gummond made a statement?"

"Actually, he made several statements when he was sent over for psychiatric evaluation," Waker replied. "According to the doctor who is checking him, he suffers from a rare psychological disorder, one of occasionally lying compulsively."

"Occasional compulsive lying?"

"Yes." Walker smiled. "In one variation of the disorder, the doc tells me, the patient lies every other statement. In the only other variation, the patient lies every third statement. The doctor can't tell yet which variation Gummond has."

"Extraordinary!" Stanwick's eyes sparkled. "Do you happen to remember what he said?"

"I think I have it here," replied Walker, extracting and flipping open his notebook. "Gummond made five statements: 1) I've never been in Big Jake's in my life. 2) I've been in Royston for the last two weeks. 3) I didn't shoot that Valenzi guy. 4) It is not true that I was in Detroit five days ago. 5) I own a gun, but it's with my sister in Chicago."

"Fascinating," murmured Stanwick distantly. "And where is Gummond now?"

"Still undergoing psych eval," said Walker. "Any thoughts?"

"One or two," Stanwick replied with a yawn. "For one, you can tell the doctor that Gummond suffers from the first variation of the disorder. For another, you can tell the chief that Gummond did the shooting."

How does Stanwick know this?

Solution on page 86.

Murder by the Wayward

A MANDA TUCKER, attorney at law, smiled and accepted a mug of tea from Thomas P. Stanwick, who then sat down across from her in his usual armchair.

"I'm glad you stopped by, Amanda," the amateur logician said genially. "I haven't seen you in a while. How've you been? And how's Roger?"

"I'm fine, thanks, Tom," she replied. "And so's the boy. He's visiting his father this week; it's spring vacation, you know."

"So it is." Stanwick grinned. "I'm glad I'm not traveling."

"It's just as well he's away. I'm tied up now with a property case I've taken over from Maryellen Beecher. In fact, I'm on my way back from a deposition. Maryellen had to leave the case now that she's representing the prime suspect in the Lubbock murder."

"Lubbock. Wasn't that the fellow shot in the parking lot of the Wayward Inn in East Frailey?" Stanwick asked.

"That's right. Do you know much about it?"

"Not as much as I'd like to."

"Then allow me," said Tucker. "Archie Lubbock, 47, was a trust administrator for a local bank. A widower, he had for two years been dating Maggie Thurston, 35, an aeronautical engineer. Last Monday evening, they met at the inn for dinner. They arrived about 7:30 in separate cars and went in together.

"Partway through the meal, they quarreled. She says she was angry because he was reluctant to visit her parents in Kentucky next summer. Witnesses say she picked up her light jacket and stormed out. He paused just long enough to extract a large bill from his wallet and throw it on the table. Then he picked up his trench coat and hurried after her.

"About 10 minutes later, a departing customer found him lying by the rear of his car, shot dead. His key case was clutched in his hand, and the blood showed that he was shot where found. His wallet was gone, as were Thurston and her car."

"Did she own a gun?"

"No record of it, for what that's worth. The police picked her up at her home the next morning for questioning. She hasn't been arrested yet but remains the prime suspect, so she has retained Maryellen as a precaution. The police theory is that she waited for Lubbock near his car, either visibly or in the cedar hedge that lines the parking lot—the shot came from that direction—and then shot him, taking his wallet as a ruse, and fled."

"Hmmm." Stanwick swallowed some tea. "Is it certain that they arrived at the same time?"

"The driver of the car parked between theirs says so. Thurston parked her car nearer the inn door. The other diners confirmed the quarrel and their departure."

"I see." Stanwick set his mug down with a decisive thump. "I'm sure any associate of yours should be able to clear Thurston. She didn't shoot Lubbock."

How does Stanwick know that Thurston is innocent?

Solution on page 90.

Death at the Clinic

"IT'S YOUR BAD LUCK, old chum," said Thomas P. Stanwick, the amateur logician, "that I recently made a special study of the Queen's Gambit Declined. That's when I found that innovation against your Cambridge Springs Defense that helped me win tonight."

Inspector Matthew Walker grunted. "Unfortunately, a working cop doesn't have time to keep up with your theoretical novelties. Good game, though."

Stanwick and Walker were relaxing in armchairs in the lounge of the Royston Chess Club following their weekly game. The windows were open to the warm evening air.

"How are Elizabeth and the boys?" asked Stanwick as he lit his pipe.

"Just fine, thanks," replied Walker. "When I left, Elizabeth was on the phone with one of her friends talking about their awful soap opera."

"'Awful soap opera' is not a very exclusive term. Which one?"

"'All My Nights.' An hour of guff. It's also popular, I've learned, in one of the best nutrition clinics in the city."

"Indeed?" Stanwick smiled and arched his eyebrows. "And how would a well-fed fellow like you know that?"

"A murder case. Dr. Mila Dixon runs a private clinic on the East End, and one of her nutritionists, Lola Alvarez, was shot to death last Wednesday."

"I see." Stanwick's face relaxed into pensiveness. "Any suspects? And what's the connection with 'All My Nights'?"

"We have three suspects, all regular clients of Lola's. Malcolm Beard, a neurosurgeon, arrived just as 'All My Nights', which begins at 1:30, was ending. He went in to Lola's consulting room and hurried out, looking pale. One of the other nutritionists, Ellen Tiffany, shopped at Rosella's, a downtown boutique, for two hours after it opened and arrived back at the clinic half an hour later. Her arrival coincided with that of Frank McGowan, a building contractor. He was there exactly as long after the noon factory whistle four blocks away sounded as he was there before it."

"When does Rosella's open?"

"Nine."

"And the third suspect?"

"A personal-injury lawyer named Arthur Workman. Our witnesses have him arriving 45 minutes after McGowan left. He stayed half an hour to an hour."

Stanwick idly twisted the tip of his brown mustache.

"Interesting," he said. "Who discovered the body?"

"Mila, at about three. A silencer had been used on the gun. Lola was lying beside a tall scale. Beneath her was a smashed clock showing 1:44, which Doc Pillsbury says is consistent with the medical evidence as the time of death. The killer wasn't necessarily the last one to arrive, since any of them might have been too scared to report the body."

"Have you made the arrest yet?"

Walker shook his head. "We're still investigating."

"Fair enough." Stanwick tapped some ashes out of his pipe. "Assuming that the killer is one of your three suspects, however, a little deduction reveals which one it is."

Who murdered Lola Alvarez?

Solution on page 87.

The Stolen War Club Caper

THOMAS P. STANWICK, the amateur logician, was particularly cheery that June morning as he sat down in his usual chair in Inspector Walker's office. Walker looked up from his paperwork in surprise.

"Why, hello, Tom," he said. "You don't often come around here on a Monday. Good to see you, though."

"Thank you. And you're right of course, Matt." Stanwick crossed his legs and began to fill his briar pipe. "I just wanted to stop by before I go on vacation. I sent off my last editing job last night—a textbook on postwar American history—and I leave for England tomorrow. A Churchill Society dinner in London, then off to see some old friends in Cambridge and hike in the Highlands. Back in three weeks."

Walker snorted. "Someday you'll have to get a real job like the rest of us."

"No doubt." Stanwick grinned. "But not today. Anyway, what's new and interesting with you?"

"Not much." Walker took a report off one of the piles of paper on his desk. "Some prankster has been busy at Royston State. Have you heard of Chief Kayoka's war club?"

"Why, yes." Stanwick puffed pensively at his pipe. "It's a very valuable 18th-century artifact kept in the college museum. I've seen it there."

"Exactly. Well, last Saturday night, someone took it from the museum and lashed it to the flagpole in front of the administration building."

Stanwick laughed heartily. "I'll bet Dean Ralph didn't take too kindly to that."

"No, he didn't. He demanded an immediate investigation by the campus police, and has just forwarded their preliminary report to me. It's a piece of garbage! You would think that, if the

41

dean wanted to put this on our plate, he would send us an intelligible report."

"It's that bad?"

"Terrible! Now, the campus police are sure the culprit was a student. They have the suspects narrowed down to three, each of whom has a connection to the museum. Any one of them could have made the unforced entry. Their names are Kelly Raposa, Eric Walton, and Jason Vokanian. Each belongs to a different secret society, one of which is something called the Mausoleum. Each also has a different major (one of which is engineering) and a different alibi."

"So far, so good," remarked Stanwick. "What's the problem?"

"Why, the fools don't identify who's who!" said Walker, angrily clutching the report. "Listen to this: the member of the Flag & Feathers Society claims to have been studying in the library that night. Of course, they neglect to mention who that is. Raposa, who is not the geography major, belongs to Alpha Gamma Quad. The Flag & Feathers person has been cleared of suspicion. Vokanian says he was bar-hopping downtown that night. Walton is the history major. Finally, the thief is not the one who claims to have been working in the computer center that night. And this is supposed to make sense?"

"May I see that?" asked Stanwick. Walker handed him the report.

"I suppose you're about to tell me," said Walker sarcastically, "that it's possible to deduce which student belongs to which society and has which major and which alibi, as well as who stole the club."

Stanwick laughed as he scanned the report.

"Your powers of prognostication, Matt, grow ever stronger. It is indeed possible, and I can tell you who's who right now."

Can you?

Solution on page 95.

The Case of the Royston Reindeer

"THE SHOT probably came from one of the boats, Inspector! There were two at the mouth of the harbor: the Dunfishin and the St. Elmo. Look for them!" An angry James Coughlin, attorney at law, stopped jabbing his finger, folded his arms, and sat back in his chair.

Across the table from him, Inspector Matthew Walker calmly picked up a sheet of paper.

"I have the ballistics report, counselor," he said. "Eleanor Freedman was shot by exactly the kind of rifle you are known to have possessed. She owned a successful hardware business and

left a large estate and no family. As her attorney and executor, you have a financial interest in her death."

Coughlin snorted.

"Innuendo! I lost my rifle on a hunting trip in Central America five years ago. Got caught in a mud slide, and barely saved my neck. My rifle is still buried there somewhere."

"Were there witnesses to that?" asked Thomas P. Stanwick, the amateur logician, who was sitting in on the interrogation.

"No. My hunting companions caught up with me afterwards."

"Let's return to the events of last Thursday, Mr. Coughlin," said Walker. "Miss Freedman was taking a New Year's Day swim in the harbor at sunrise with 18 other members of the Royston Reindeer, who take that cold swim every year. You say you witnessed the swim from the 11th floor of your office building, about a block west of the harbor."

"That's right. I was high enough to have a direct view, and it was a clear morning."

"And you were working on New Year's Day?"

"I had an important deposition to prepare. No one else was there."

Half an hour later, Walker and Stanwick were down the hall in Walker's office.

"It's rather inconvenient for him that he can't produce his rifle for testing or any witnesses to corroborate his alibi," remarked Stanwick.

"Yes," said Walker. "We're trying to trace those boats he mentioned. Because the swimmers were moving around, we can't be sure what direction or height the shot came from."

"The Royston Reindeer?" Stanwick smiled. " I knew reindeer could fly this time of year, but didn't know they could swim! At least Dasher and Dancer would live up to their names if thrown into icy water, no doubt. Anything interesting in the victim's effects?"

Walker shook his head. "She left her clothes, a robe, a towel, and her purse in the locker room of their clubhouse, as the others did. Oddly, she was the only one wearing a white bath cap, which made her stand out. No shot was heard. The others thought she had had a heart attack or a seizure in the water."

"And Coughlin's office window would allow him to see the swimmers and the boats?"

"Oh, sure. The window opens, too, if you get my drift."

"I think I do." Stanwick idly fingered the tip of his droopy mustache. "I also think that Coughlin's alibi is a crock."

How does Stanwick know that Coughlin is lying?

Solution on page 92.

Memorial Day Mischief

Thomas P. Stanwick was enjoying the annual Memorial Day festivities in his hometown of Baskerville.

The pancake breakfast in the armory had given the amateur logician a chance to catch up on local gossip. The parade up Main Street had started promptly at 10, and the flags, the veterans, the militia members in their colonial uniforms, and the school bands looked and sounded crisp. Civic leaders and town officials, and of course the Veteran of Honor, smiled and waved as they slowly marched down the street. The parade would be followed by a chicken barbecue in the playground.

Stanwick was viewing the parade from the sidewalk just outside Ollie's Army & Navy store. Just as a crack riflery unit was passing in front of him, the parade paused. For two minutes, in absolute silence, the riflers spun and tossed their rifles in compli-

cated and exquisitely timed patterns. When they concluded, the band behind them struck up a march and the parade proceeded, to cheers and enthusiastic applause from the crowd.

A moment later, Stanwick heard a bellow of rage from the store just behind him. Entering it, Stanwick found the flushed-faced owner, Ollie Fortison, standing behind his sales counter holding an empty cash drawer from the register. Fortison, a burly former drill sergeant, glowered at four startled customers.

"What's wrong, Ollie?" asked Stanwick, walking up to him.

"This is what's wrong!" Fortison exclaimed, holding out the cash drawer. "This had over $300 in it five minutes ago, and now the bills are gone!"

"Please tell me what happened."

Fortison drew a long breath.

"It's simple enough, Tom," he said. "As you know, I stay open on Memorial Day until the parade is over, to sell flags or any last-minute items. I had just opened my cash drawer to sort my bills

when the crowd outside grew quiet. Then I remembered that that out-of-town rifle unit was going to put on a show.

"I wanted to see it, so like a fool I left my cash drawer open and came to the window. At least a few of these customers did the same, but I didn't notice which ones. You could have heard a firing pin drop during the rifle display. When it was over, I came back to the counter and found the money gone!"

"And I heard your reaction on the sidewalk outside." Stanwick suppressed a grin. "Call the station, Ollie. And," he added, turning to the others, "I suggest that the rest of you remain until an officer arrives for your statements."

Stanwick was acquainted with two of the customers. One was Ellen Lilliott, a pretty brunette dressed in a tank top, shorts, and strap clogs, who owned a flower stand in town. The other was Paul Breen, a sandy-haired but balding executive in his 50's. Breen was dressed in an unholidaylike suit and wing tip shoes. The two other customers were both young men, one with a military crew cut who was dressed in fatigues and boots, the other in a T-shirt, shorts, and sneakers.

A careful look around the store revealed nothing out of place to Stanwick. On display were clothes, camping goods, military paraphernalia, and various knickknacks. The hardwood floor was spit-and-polish as usual.

As soon as the sergeant had banged down the phone, Stanwick turned to him.

"Ollie," he said quietly, "could anyone have left the store since the theft?"

"Impossible! There's only the one door, and its bell is in working order. You heard it when you came in. And no one else has been in here this morning."

"In that case," said Stanwick even more quietly, "make sure none of them leaves before the police arrive. Especially..."

Whom does Stanwick suspect of the theft, and why?

Solution on page 86.

The Phony Faith Healer

ANNIE TYNSDALE was a young, pretty Englishwoman whom Thomas P. Stanwick, the amateur logician, befriended while he was a graduate student at Cambridge University. After he returned to New England and settled into his Baskerville bungalow, she became the proprietress of a small candy shop in Cambridge. They corresponded regularly, and whenever Stanwick visited Cambridge, he made a point of seeing her.

One of his letters ran this way:

"Dear Annie,

"Thanks for your newsy letter of the 14th. Old Gordon is kind to ask about me when he visits your shop. I did him a small favor back in student days when I recovered his stolen gold pen set, and he's never got over it.

"I'm pretty busy right now finishing up a high school geometry textbook. That should be done in about two weeks. My next assignment will be to edit a textbook on the Civil War — American, that is.

"Remember that time we attended a demonstration given in London by a phony faith healer? Well, I thought of you last week when I attended a similar demonstration in Royston. Matt Walker mentioned some time ago that the police were suspicious of Joseph Howsham, a self-proclaimed faith healer and reputed con man who has always managed to stay barely within the law. When I heard that Howsham would be giving a demonstration at Mennows Hall last week, I drove into Royston to see his act.

49

"Quite an act it was, too! The hall was full. Howsham, fully bearded and dressed in purple robes, dramatically recounted a few of his past exploits and then asked that those ready to be healed come forward.

"His first 'poor unfortunate' was a middle-aged man claiming to have been blind since age 20. Howsham had him kneel. He looked up, muttered some unintelligible incantations, and passed his hands over the man's head. Lifting the man to his feet, he put his hand over the man's eyes for a moment and then removed it. The man blinked a few times, then cried, 'I can see again!'

"'What color are my robes?' asked Howsham.

"'Purple!' the man responded.

"Howsham turned the man toward the audience, raised his robed arms, and cried 'Hallelujah! He can see!'

"The now-seeing man embraced Howsham in joy and stumbled out of the hall in an apparent daze while most of the audience cheered.

"Next to come before Howsham was a man who, according to a woman with him, had been stone deaf since birth. He had learned to read lips, however, as well as to speak somewhat, so he obeyed Howsham's instruction to kneel. The passes and incantations followed. Howsham then lifted him to his feet, placed his hands briefly on the man's ears, stepped back, and asked if he could hear. The man looked startled, then broke into a smile.

"'Yes!' he cried.

"Howsham turned him toward the audience and, uplifting his face and arms again, exclaimed 'Hallelujah! He is healed!'

"'Yes, I am healed!' cried the man, who turned to thank Howsham profusely and then left the stage.

"While the audience cheered, I left the hall. I had seen enough to know conclusively that Howsham was a fake."

How did Stanwick know Howsham was a fake?

Solution on page 88

Sabotage at Centipore

THE FOURTH FLOOR of the Centipore building, which housed the Engineering division, seldom had visitors. The medical membranes produced by Centipore were designed there, so the corporate security chief, Abraham Freedman, kept Engineering a restricted area.

Some tampering with a sensitive computer disk, however, had brought two visitors to the fourth floor. Inspector Matthew Walker and Thomas P. Stanwick were in the office of Sylvia DiCampli, the vice-president of Engineering.

"The disk contains plans for a valuable membrane prototype, Inspector," DiCampli said. "It's kept in the storage room down the hall. The disk was fine when used last Wednesday, the 11th, but was found to be altered last Friday, the 13th. Harry Miller, the senior engineer who discovered the problem, reported it to me. I immediately confirmed it and reported it to Lester Parke, the executive vice-president of operations. He called your people."

"Sergeant Hatch tells me that the door to the storage room was unforced," said Walker. "Therefore it was accessed by the swipe of a magnetic card. Please tell me who had access to that room."

"Besides myself and Harry Miller, that would be two other senior engineers, Tom Donlan and Chris Delaney, and Mr. Parke. Tom is new here, though, so for now he can get access to the room only with verification by one of the others."

"Couldn't Mr. Freedman authorize access for someone else?" asked Stanwick.

"Technically, yes," DiCampli replied, "but that would be highly irregular. Besides, he was laid up with the flu all last week, and conducted no business."

"I'd like another look at the room," said Walker, standing up.

A moment later, the three of them were in the small storage room. The walls were lined with shelves of floppy disk containers. DiCampli pointed out the container with the altered disk, which sat on a separate side shelf. A computer terminal rested on a small table against the center wall.

"Is the altered disk usually kept on that shelf?" asked Stanwick.

"That's right," replied DiCampli.

"And it was not altered on this terminal?"

"Correct. This terminal makes a note on its hard drive whenever it is used. We have verified the normal use on the 11th and the use on the 13th, when Harry discovered the problem. The disk was not used here between those times."

"You also told my sergeant that using the disk on another computer would require a decryption code," said Walker.

"Yes, and the code was changed on the 9th. It's issued automatically to senior engineers, and is available to myself and higher-ups through Freedman."

"What damage to the company, Ms. DiCampli, could have resulted from the alteration of the disk?" asked Stanwick.

"It could have been worse. The alteration was discovered just in time to prevent a false patent application and costly failures in testing. Our competitors would have loved a delay in the discovery."

A short while later, Stanwick and Walker were eating lunch in the company cafeteria.

"Industrial espionage!" remarked Stanwick. "You don't often get those cases."

"True!" replied Walker with a rueful smile. "The chief still has me working as an Inspector Without Portfolio. It keeps my work varied."

"Anything interesting that you haven't told DiCampli?"

"In fact, yes." Walker leaned forward and spoke softly. "I have strong evidence that one of Centipore's competitors—one 10 times its size—selected, approached, and bribed at least one Centipore employee. We don't know which employee, though."

"Ah!" Stanwick took a pen and a pocket pad from his shirt pocket. "In that case, if all that DiCampli has told us checks out, I believe I can jot down who is responsible for the alteration of the disk."

Who altered the Centipore disk?

Solution on page 90.

The Bracken Park Incident

"SHE SAYS she never saw who attacked her," said Inspector Walker. "I've just come from the hospital. She's still pretty groggy, though, and may remember more later."

The inspector and Thomas P. Stanwick, the amateur logician, were striding briskly that crisp November morning through the streets of Royston toward Bracken Park. Earlier that morning, Alison Vaneer, a beautician in her early 30's, had been hit on the head and robbed while jogging through the park.

"When was she found?" asked Stanwick.

"About 8:30, by another jogger, just where the path passes a clump of trees. She was attacked a little after 7:00, just at daybreak. The money belt she wore around her stomach had been taken, and she was suffering from a concussion. For such chilly weather, she wasn't wearing much: a T-shirt, a tennis skirt, jacket with a reflector, a Harvard sweatshirt. And a baseball cap."

"Ah, a sedentary fellow like you wouldn't appreciate how warm some exercise can keep one," remarked Stanwick wryly.

Walker snorted. "And you would?"

They stopped by a news kiosk several yards from the south gate to the park.

"She entered the park through here," Walker said. "It's her usual route." With a flash of his badge, Walker introduced himself to the news dealer, Oscar Kramer.

"Did you see a woman jogger go into the park this morning?" he asked.

"A few, actually," Kramer answered. "Which one?"

"The one with the Harvard sweatshirt," said Stanwick.

"Oh, yeah. Around seven, just as I was starting to open up. She's gone by every morning for the last couple of weeks, just like clockwork. Why?"

"She was attacked and robbed in the park," replied Walker impassively. "Did you see any suspicious persons enter or leave the park this way this morning?"

Kramer shook his head. "No, sir."

"Thank you," said Walker. "Sergeant Hatch will be along shortly to take your statement." He and Stanwick resumed their walk.

"Hatch is still at the crime scene," Walker told Stanwick as they entered the park. "It's about 50 yards up this way."

"I suggest he question Kramer carefully," said Stanwick with a frown. "That newsdealer could easily enough have anticipated Miss Vaneer's time and route, and lain in wait for her. He also knows more about this crime than he told us—no doubt of that!"

Why does Stanwick suspect the newsdealer of the crime?

Solution on page 87.

55

The Case of the Bulgarian Diamonds

THE POLYGRAPH EXAMINATION ROOM at Royston Police head-quarters was conveniently fitted with a one-way mirror. In a small room behind this mirror stood Inspector Matthew Walker and his friend Thomas P. Stanwick, who was taking a break from his freelance editing to observe a slice of a criminal investigation.

"You may have seen something in the paper of the Bulgarian Diamond Mining Company securities scam," said Walker. "Over half a million 'invested' dollars were stolen. Of course, there was no such company."

"And these four were involved?" asked Stanwick, peering through the glass into the polygraph room.

"That's right. Louis Lambert, Diane Sorensen, Morty Cameron, and John Thorpe ran the whole operation. One of the men was the salesman, another of the four printed the phony stock certificates, another kept the books, and the fourth acted as the banker, depositing and withdrawing the funds. We're questioning them now about their roles in the scam."

As Stanwick and Walker listened, the four suspects were given polygraph examinations. Each made two statements.

"I was the bookkeeper," declared Lambert. "You know what? Thorpe was the bookkeeper too!" He cackled with laughter.

"Lambert was not the banker," said Cameron. "I printed the certificates."

"Lambert wasn't the printer," Sorensen said. "The salesman was Thorpe."

"Either Diane or Morty kept the books," said Thorpe. "Diane doesn't know a thing about printing."

It was soon apparent that the four suspects would say no more, so Stanwick, who had been taking notes, departed. He returned the next day to visit Walker in his office. He found Walker glaring at the report of the polygraph examiner.

"I can't believe it!" Walker roared. "The polygraph is acting irregularly again. I'm told that each suspect made one true statement and one false statement, but that we can't tell which is which! I've got to persuade the chief to budget a new machine."

Stanwick laughed heartily.

"I hear that polygraphs are notoriously unreliable," he said. "If that report is true, though, a little logic can determine which statements were true, which were false, and who played what role in the scam!"

Who did what in the Bulgarian Diamond Mining Company?

Solution on page 94.

The Case of the Bulgonian Spy

THE DUCKS IN ST. JAMES PARK eagerly accepted the bread crumbs Thomas P. Stanwick offered as he sat on a bench chatting with his old friend Inspector Gilbert Bodwin. Stanwick was in London for a week to relax and attend a symposium on logic education. He and Bodwin were discussing crime, as usual.

"Then there's my spy case," remarked Bodwin. "The Yard is assisting DI5 (the old MI5, like your CIA, of course) in recovering stolen Ministry of Defence plans for a submarine firing sequence scrambler. We've established that they were taken by someone at the embassy of the Free Democratic People's Republic of North Bulgonia, which has for years been angling for military technology to use against the genuinely free Republic of South Bulgonia."

"Submarine plans?" Stanwick looked puzzled. "Aren't both countries landlocked?"

"Yes, but they share a large lake, and maintain freshwater sub fleets."

Stanwick laughed. "And how were the plans taken?"

"A senior Defence official, Warren Perry, very carelessly took away a copy of the plans and left them exposed in the bar of a hotel, where they disappeared. He has since been reprimanded. We believe that the thief was one of two North Bulgonian embassy employees, Vlado Impalus or Boris Gulkovo. Both were in the bar that evening."

"Indeed? Please go on."

Bodwin grunted and pulled out his official notebook. "We've interviewed the bartender, the waitress, the hotel concierge, and several others," he said. "Perry arrived at the bar at 6:30 P.M. with a woman, took a table, and ordered cocktails. They sat at drinks for an hour and a half, then the woman left. Perry opened his briefcase and worked for an hour. Then his phone beeper went off, and he was gone for a quarter of an hour answering it. Fifteen minutes after his return, he noticed the plans missing and raised the alarm.

"Impalus arrived at the bar with a friend half an hour after Perry. They drank gin-and-tonics at a table for an hour and a quarter until the friend left. A quarter of an hour later, Impalus went to the gents', returning after another quarter of an hour. Sometime in the next half-hour, he left.

"The other one, Gulkovo," Bodwin continued, "arrived at the bar alone half an hour after Impalus arrived, took a table, and drank a whiskey and soda. After three-quarters of an hour, he went to the gents' for a quarter of an hour. A quarter of an hour after his return, he went to the lounge, bought a paper, and read it there for half an hour. Then he returned to the bar briefly, picked up his coat, and left."

"Hmm." Stanwick threw his remaining bread crumbs into the pond, where several ducks swarmed upon them. "Is Perry sure that the plans were in his case when he arrived?"

"Yes. He saw them when he began working on his papers. We have ample evidence, incidentally, that he is guilty only of incompetence, not espionage."

"In that case," said Stanwick, standing up and stretching, "the identity of the spy is clearly deducible. How about some lunch?"

Who is the spy?

Solution on page 90.

One Morning at the Festival

THE VILLAGE OF Knordwyn in Northumbria, England, was cel-
ebrating its annual Queen Anne Festival. For several August
days, people from around the shire came to enjoy craft displays,
athletic competitions, farm shows, and cooking and music contests.

Also attending the festival was Thomas P. Stanwick, the amateur logician. He visited the village every year or two, and found
Knordwynians invariably intriguing: about half were lifelong
liars, and the rest were lifelong truthtellers. Conversations with
them were thus real tests of his skill at deduction.

On the second festival day, Stanwick arrived at the grounds early to see the pigs. He was curious to see a particularly hefty specimen named Miss Porky Pine (because of her prickly disposition, according to a wag at the village pub). When he reached the stalls, however, he found hers empty and her owner, Ian Craigmore, angrily questioning three men and a woman. Upon seeing Stanwick, Craigmore turned to him.

"Tom, my lad," he sputtered, "someone stole Miss Porky Pine from her stall last night. It must have been one thief: she is nervous and squeals loudly if two try to handle her."

"And you suspect these four?"

"Yes. Charles Hagman, Thomas Leary, and Dora Glasker are festival attendants, and Louis Parrella was cooking a suspiciously early barbecue not far from the festival grounds, so I brought him over. All four are from the village."

Stanwick knew Craigmore to be a villager and a truthteller. Turning to the suspects, he asked if they could tell him anything about the theft.

"Louis never attends the festival," said Hagman. "Also, Thomas and Dora are not both truthtellers."

"Dora stole the pig," announced Leary. "She and Louis are both liars."

Glasker cleared her throat angrily. "Neither Charles nor Thomas is the thief," she said. "Louis attends the festival every other year."

"Either Dora or Thomas is a liar," stated Parrella. "The thief, however, is not Charles or Dora."

Stanwick smiled pleasantly.

"In an admittedly indirect way," he said, "you've been very helpful. And now," he continued, turning to one of them, "perhaps you could tell us why you stole the portly pig."

Who stole Miss Porky Pine?

Solution on page 89.

Chief Ryan Pays a Call

CHIEF WILLIAM RYAN of the Baskerville Police was exchanging local gossip with Thomas P. Stanwick one afternoon in the living room of Stanwick's bungalow. Stanwick's black Labrador, Rufus, slept peacefully in a patch of sunlight.

"I think the Sherman lad will turn out all right," concluded the chief, a taciturn man with thinning hair. "I had a long talk with him. He won't go wrong again."

"That's good to hear, Chief," said Stanwick. "The Shermans are a fine family. Do you have any interesting investigations going on these days?"

"Actually, we do. Three local stores—Fine Jewels, Harrigan's

Hardware, and the Gasco Mart—have been robbed by a small gang of teenagers over the last two months. The same gang has hit stores in two other nearby towns. The four teens in the gang are students from the Baskerville and Royston high schools, so we've been running a joint investigation with the Royston police."

"Who's in charge at the Royston end?" asked Stanwick. "Matt Walker?"

"No. Inspector Martinez."

Stanwick nodded. "She's very capable."

"Anyway, we've identified the four. The Baskerville students are Lisa Janison and Tony Aronisi. Fred Wynant and Joyce Bobbin are from Royston. We have them under surveillance, but we want to learn more about them before we make any arrests.

"We especially want to learn what nicknames they call each other, and how they rank themselves within the group," the chief went on. "One of them is called Muscle. The one in charge is of course called Leader. Bobbin, we find, outranks Wynant but is not Leader. Aronisi is called Driver. (Guess what his job is!) The one called Weapons, who is not Wynant, is ranked just below Leader. We also know that Driver is not the lowest-ranked position. We need more than these bits and pieces, though, to sort out who is who in what order of rank. Only then will we be ready to take them to court."

Stanwick smiled and slowly filled his pipe.

"I've been up to my elbows in a geometry manuscript all day," he remarked genially, "and I thought your visit, no offense, would give me a break from deductive reasoning. Alas, no! I think I can prove, in fact, that the 'bits and pieces' you cite are enough to give you the information you want."

Which gang member has what nickname and rank?

Solution on page 92.

The Powers' Predicament

"THANK YOU KINDLY," said Thomas P. Stanwick, leaning forward in his chair to accept more tea and another piece of cake from Genevieve Hardis. "You must be looking forward to seeing your family next week for Thanksgiving."

"Yes, indeed, my boy," replied Ron Hardis, a grin creasing his strong jaw. "We're going out to Charlie's, in upstate New York."

"Our three children and their families will all be there," Gen Hardis said as she sat down.

Stanwick was in the living room visiting the elderly but vigorous Hardises. "Thanksgiving came on fast this year," he said. "Pretty soon, every corner will have a Santa ringing a bell."

"That's right," said Gen. "We give to a few charities, and the Christmas appeals have already begun to arrive in the mail. One came the other day from an outfit we never heard of, 'Family Help Today.'"

"Hmm. That's new to me, too," said Stanwick. "May I see it?"

"Here it is," said Ron, taking a letter from an end table and handing it to Stanwick. "It's from someone named Arnold Creelman, 'regional coordinator,' asking for help for a homeless family."

Stanwick settled back to read the letter.

"Dear RON HARDIS:

"This holiday season, a generous citizen like you will want to assist your needy neighbors in BASKERVILLE. Let me introduce you to the Powers family. Frank Powers, a former Navy flier, is now disabled and can do only odd jobs. He, his wife Maryann, who is unemployed, and their two children, Marjorie, 11, and Robbie, 8, are living in their station wagon, with their few goods piled in the back.

"In spite of their difficulties, Marjorie and Robbie attend school and do their homework in the BASKERVILLE public library. They sneak showers in the school gym when they can. At night, the family sleeps in the car with the heat on to keep warm.

"Can you help the members of the Powers family get back on their feet? They distrust homeless shelters, which you will agree are not good places for children. RON HARDIS, your contribution this holiday season will be much appreciated."

Stanwick smiled and put down the letter.

"How charmingly personal," he said. "I suggest you find worthier causes for your giving. On at least two counts, this appeal is a fraud."

How does Stanwick know that the charity appeal is a fraud?

Solution on page 86.

An Idyll Day in Edinburgh

THOMAS P. STANWICK, the amateur logician, was on vacation in Edinburgh and had spent most of an idyllic autumn afternoon browsing in musty bookshops. Shortly before dusk, he visited a small shop off a crooked lane. He had just opened a book on medieval Scottish theology when he heard the sharp voice of the elderly shop owner directed at a goateed man at the door.

"Excuse me, sir," said the owner, "but did you not forget to pay me for the Anderson book in your hand?"

"Why, no, sir," replied the customer, stepping back inside. "I bought this last week at another shop—for less than your price, I may add—and had it with me when I came in here."

"No, no, I'm sure this is mine," said the owner, walking up to the customer and pointing toward his shelves. "You see the gap in that shelf there? I have only the one copy, and have not sold it."

"You must be mistaken, sir. Perhaps you simply forgot selling it."

"I think not. Excuse me." The owner turned over the cover. "Ah! As you can see, there are erasure marks in the corner of the inside page, where I always note the price in pencil. You have erased it!"

"All bookshops put the price there," snapped the customer. "I erased it after I got the book home last week."

"Have you a receipt for this?"

"Not anymore. I threw it away days ago. Did you not see me enter with the book?"

"No, but my back was turned when you came in, I must confess."

"Well, then," said the customer, turning away. "I'll be on my way."

"I beg your pardon," said Stanwick. He walked up and addressed the customer. "It would be cumbersome to call in the police, who could search you for an eraser, possibly on a pencil, or search the shop for one you might have discarded. You have already incriminated yourself, however, so perhaps you would be willing to make restitution to this gentleman privately instead."

How did the customer incriminate himself?

Solution on page 90.

Room at the Inn

DUSK WAS GATHERING as Thomas P. Stanwick, the amateur logician, arrived in Knordwyn at the end of a 15-mile hike. He was fond of visiting the tiny Northumbrian village when he was on vacation in England. About half its inhabitants always lied, and the rest always told the truth. His conversations with them were thus stimulating exercises in deduction.

With a sigh of relief, Stanwick threw off his backpack and sat down heavily on a bench by the village green. His immediate concern was to find a room for the night. Three villagers were passing by just then, and he hailed them.

"Excuse me," he asked, "but are any rooms available at the Grey Boar Inn tonight?"

"Yes, there are," said the first villager.

"Either no rooms are available," said the second villager, "or he and I are both liars."

"Either two of us are liars," added the third villager, "or the first fellow is telling the truth."

"Thank you," said Stanwick with a weary smile. He was used to the sometimes wildly indirect answers of the villagers. These three had said enough, however, for him to deduce who was lying and, more important, whether there was room at the inn.

Who is lying? Is there room at the inn?

Solution on page 94.

The Prom Date Puzzle

Thomas P. Stanwick placed a can of soda and a bowl of chips on the small table beside his seated visitor and then sat down in his usual armchair, popping the tab on his own can of cola as he did so.

"I'm glad you dropped by, Brian," he said. Brian Capello and his parents were neighbors of Stanwick's, and he had known them for years. "How's school going?"

"Not bad, Mr. S.," replied the teenager. "Only about six weeks to go. The prom is in three weeks."

"Have you got a date yet?"

"Naw. My pals and I haven't decided how to pair up."

Stanwick looked puzzled. "This is a group decision?"

"Yeah. Harv, George, Roger, and I hang with Marlene, Lizbeth, Deb, and Annette. Just friends, but we want to pair up for the prom. All us guys but George want to take a girl who isn't taller than us; George, who's five-ten, doesn't care. I'm five-nine, Harv is five-seven, and Roger is five-eight. Marlene is six feet, Lizbeth is five-seven, Deb is five-eight, and Annette is five-five."

"I see." Stanwick suddenly felt very old.

"Each of the girls, on the other hand, wants to go with a guy with a lower grade point average, so that she isn't seen by the prom crowd as a dumb babe. Annette has a 3.5, the highest of us all. Marlene has a 2.5, Lizbeth has a 3.1, and Deb has a 3.4. Among us guys, I have a 3.0, Roger has a 2.9, Harv has a 3.3, and George has a 2.0."

Stanwick took a swig of cola and then scribbled on a pad of paper.

"It seems to me," he said, "that you have a couple of possible pairing arrangements that would meet those requirements."

"But there's one more thing," continued Brian. "Roger wants to take a girl who likes to slow-dance, which Marlene and Deb don't. I tell you, Mr. S., we've been hashing this around for a couple of weeks and are about ready to forget the whole thing."

"No need to do that, my lad!" said Stanwick cheerily. "Group-date negotiations for the prom are new since I was in high school a thousand years ago, but with the help of a little logic, I believe I can show you the one pairing arrangement that will meet everyone's requirements."

What pairing arrangement will work?

Solution on page 92.

Stanwick Solves a Pie Puzzle

O N THE FIRST SATURDAY of each May, Baskerville held its annual Craft & Bake Fair on the large, open playground behind the elementary school. In colorful booths and tents were displayed handmade stitchery and sculpture, along with home-baked breads, cookies, cakes, and pies.

Thomas P. Stanwick always enjoyed the chance to buy delectables and see friends and neighbors at the fair. This year, however, an investigation in Royston kept him from the fairgrounds until late in the afternoon. Once there, he visited several displays. His last stop was a large, open tent that had several tables of baked goods.

Three elderly ladies named Frieda, Gertie, and Hazel were behind one table talking busily among themselves. The table had a cherry pie in the center and a blueberry pie in the back right corner. Stanwick knew all three women and greeted them cheerily.

"Good day, ladies!" he said. "Only two pies left, I see. Whose are they?"

"Why, Thomas," replied Frieda, "we were just trying to remember that ourselves, so that the unsold pies can go home with their bakers. We each made an apple, a blueberry, and a cherry, you see, but didn't label them by owner. The sale money went into the charity pot."

"So you had nine pies, and sold seven," said Stanwick. "How were they placed on the table?"

"We had three rows of three pies each," replied Gertie. "Each row had one of each type of pie. Only one or two of my pies were sold."

"Each of us had one pie in the front row," said Hazel. "Gertie had two pies in the middle row, I remember. I also remember that my apple and my blueberry were sold. I'm not sure about my cherry."

Stanwick chuckled as he took out his wallet.

"The question is moot," he said, "since I will buy the two remaining pies. They look delicious. With the help of a little logic, however, I can tell you who baked them."

Who baked which remaining pies?

Solution on page 95.

73

Stanwick at Chartwell

THOMAS P. STANWICK had always been a great admirer of Winston Churchill. When traveling in England in the summertime, the amateur logician enjoyed visiting Chartwell, Churchill's home near Westerham. Over the years, he had become acquainted with several of the National Trust staffers who maintained it.

On this occasion, Stanwick was sitting on a bench overlooking the estate's lake and the green Kent hillsides, chatting with Niles Archer. A soft-spoken man with thick-framed glasses, Archer was one of the Chartwell administrators.

"Has Chartwell had a good flow of visitors this summer, Niles?" asked Stanwick.

"Oh, yes," Archer replied. "We've been busy. We've also had an unusual number of special tours. The Churchill family is especially interested in these, so one of my duties is to prepare a weekly report on them. This week, unfortunately, my report will be a bit patchy."

"No special tours this week?"

"Oh, no, we've had five already. The bad luck is, I have mislaid my notes on the history club that visited us yesterday afternoon. I do remember that there were four members: Elaine Thompson, Albert Martin, Bill Colville, and Ellen Pearman. They came from Oldham, Epping, Dundee, and Woodford, though I forget in which order. One was a bricklayer, another was an historian, another was a novelist, and the fourth was a landscape painter, but again I forget which was which."

"That's remarkable!" Stanwick laughed. "How appropriate that such a group should visit Chartwell. Their last names are those of important assistants to Churchill. They come from towns that Churchill represented in Parliament. And their occupations reflect some of Churchill's own occupations and hobbies."

"Why, so they do!" Archer smiled. "Thank you, Thomas. That had not occurred to me. Those points can help salvage my report."

"Can you remember anything more about the group?"

"Well, let me see. The woman from Dundee was neither the painter nor the bricklayer. Mr. Martin, of Epping, despised writing of any kind. Mrs. Pearman was not, I believe, from Woodford. The historian was a bachelor from Oldham. And I gained the distinct understanding that Miss Thompson did not work with a trowel."

"Well done, Niles!" exclaimed Stanwick with a grin. "With a little deduction, your report can yet be made complete. If you'll join me over a cup of tea, I'll jot down who did what where."

Can you match the visitors with their occupations and towns?

Solution on page 92.

The Tale of the Generous Rajah

AN ARMCHAIR in the reading room of the Baskerville Public Library proved too comfortable a place for Thomas P. Stanwick at four o'clock on a warm afternoon. His eyes slid closed, his head slumped to his chest, and the book slipped from his fingers to the floor.

The head librarian, who had seen these symptoms before, walked quietly over to the amateur logician and gently shook his shoulder.

"Mr. Stanwick! You haven't fallen asleep, have you, sir?" she asked.

Stanwick snapped to alertness.

"What?" he said. "Oh, hello, Mrs. Mitten. Good Lord, I wasn't snoring, was I?"

"No, no. I caught you in time."

"Thank you." Stanwick sheepishly picked up the book. "It's no reflection on what I was reading. Have you seen the memoirs of Morton Henry Stanley? He was a British explorer who traveled from Bombay across the Thar Desert to the northern reaches of India in the early 1800's."

"No, I don't think I've heard the name." Intrigued, the librarian sat down in the chair beside Stanwick's and examined the book closely.

"Stanley had many interesting adventures," Stanwick went on. "In one, he missed an excellent chance of gaining a large fortune in precious stones."

"Do go on," the librarian said.

Stanwick settled back in his chair and toyed with the tip of his droopy mustache.

"Well, as you probably know," he recounted, "India in those days had many independent kingdoms, or *raji*, each ruled by a fierce rajah. During one of his journeys, Stanley was captured by one of these rajahs. The rajah found his prisoner to be a fascinating conversationalist. (Stanley was a gifted linguist and knew several Indian dialects.) They discussed local politics and world events, and played many games of chess.

"That night the rajah presided over an elaborate dinner, which was, according to his custom, to have been followed by the execution of the trespasser. The rajah, however, announced that he would give Stanley an opportunity to leave the raj unharmed and even wealthy.

"Three large chests were brought in to the center of the dining hall. Each was lavishly bound and secured by a huge lock. A besotted servant then stumbled in carrying three signs, one picturing a diamond, another picturing a ruby, and the third picturing an emerald. The fellow first put the emerald sign on the first trunk. After a confused pause, he then took that sign off the first trunk and put it on the second trunk. Finally, after some fumbling, he put the diamond sign on the first trunk and the ruby sign on the third trunk. Then he staggered out.

"'You must forgive my servant,' laughed the rajah, turning to his guest of honor. 'He has taken a little too much hashish today. I am afraid that in none of his attempts did he succeed in putting the correct sign on the correct chest. Nonetheless, one chest does contain diamonds, another contains rubies, and another emeralds.

"'Each chest has a rather complicated lock. Here is a golden lockpick. I will give you five minutes to open one of the chests. Seeing its contents should enable you to divine the contents of all three chests. If you succeed in divining this, you may have all three chests and their contents, and safe passage to the border. If you fail, I fear I must proceed with the execution. You may begin.'

"Stanley needed no further prompting. Snatching up the lockpick, he hurried over to the three chests, paused briefly, and then began furiously picking at the lock of the middle chest, the one with the emerald sign. As the rajah chuckled quietly, Stanley muttered to himself and wrestled with the lock. Beads of sweat glistened on his forehead as the rajah called time. With a curse, Stanley flung the pick to the ground and glared at the still impregnable lock.

"The rajah laughed heartily at the spectacle of the explorer's fury and frustration.

"'Such a pity!' he exclaimed. 'I fear that the lock was too stubborn for you.'

"'Just tell me what is in one of these chests, good rajah,' said Stanley, 'and I will indeed tell you what is in the other two.'

"'I am sure you could, my friend,' replied the rajah. 'But fear

not. You have entertained me well today, so I will spare your life and reward you for your company.'

"The rajah then made good on his word by giving our relieved hero a small bagful of precious stones and a mounted escort to the border of the raj."

Stanwick grinned slyly. Mrs. Mitten, who had a weakness for tales of adventure in exotic lands, remained lost in thought for a moment.

"It's a shame that he couldn't open the lock," she said at last. "I think I see how he could then have deduced the contents of all three chests, if all the signs were put on wrong."

"Quite true!" said Stanwick with a laugh. "Poor Stanley, however, was not quite astute enough to guess the real cause of the rajah's amusement. If only the brave explorer had been a little

more alert, he might have realized that he had the power to 'divine' the contents of all three chests without touching the lockpick at all."

How could Stanley have done this?

Solution on page 88.

The Case of the Contentious Cows

WITH A PACK on his back and a staff in his hand, Thomas P. Stanwick strode down a gently sloping hill as he followed Route 221. The amateur logician, weary after many weeks of editing a long geometry textbook and helping Inspector Walker solve crimes, was enjoying a summer walking tour in Vermont. He was now about 12 miles from the Greenfield Inn, where he would spend the night.

As Stanwick approached the bottom of the hill, he observed several cows behind a gate on the left and a farm lad staring at them from the road side of the gate. Some of the cows were black, some were brown, and all had white patches. The boy, who was about 16, wore a dirty corduroy cap, a T-shirt, and a pair of old jeans. He continued to scowl at the cows as Stanwick came up to him.

"Good morning," said Stanwick, pausing to chat. "Fine weather. Time to bring the cows across?"

The boy grunted. "Ain't quite that easy, though," he muttered.

"No? Why not?"

"These are peculiar cows, Mister. The black ones are real nasty, and will butt and bite the brown ones if they outnumber 'em and I ain't right there."

"Can't you just bring them all across at once?"

"Nope. Only two at a time. Gotta hold 'em by the collar or they trot away up the road."

"They are peculiar cows!" remarked Stanwick with a grin. "You have four black ones and three brown ones, I see."

"I've been tryin' for an hour to get these cows across," the boy blurted out angrily, "and every way I try, I leave more black cows than brown cows alone on one side of the road or the other! Can you give me a hand, Mister?"

"I'm afraid I'm not much good at handling cows myself," Stanwick said. "I think I can show you a way, though, to get the cows across without leaving more black ones than brown ones together unattended."

How can the cows be brought safely across the road?

Solution on page 95.

Babies for the Bulletin

"**G**OOD MORNING, LOUISE!" exclaimed Thomas P. Stanwick as he and Rufus entered the church office. "Mind if a man and his dog drop by to say hello?"

Louise Muller, the church secretary, looked up with a start and smiled.

"Why, not at all," she replied. "It's nice to see you, Tom. And you too, Rufus." She patted the black Labrador as he sat beside her.

"I'll try not to sneeze," Stanwick said with a grin. "With so many slips of paper on your desk, any air disturbance might delay your finishing the bulletin for a month!"

"That could hardly make it worse right now," said Muller with a small sigh. "It's so embarrassing, Tom! Four babies were born to members within the last couple of weeks, on March 27, March 30, April 2, and April 4. Two are little girls (Jennifer and Lucile) and two are little boys (Frederick and Wolfgang). I'm supposed to put their full names, birthdates, and birth weights in the bulletin, but my notes got mixed up. And I would feel silly to have to go to the parents about it! But I suppose I'll have to."

"I see." Stanwick sat down in a chair beside the desk and looked over the note slips. "Are these the last names? Sartorius, Shirley, Wagner, and Lee?"

"That's right. And the weights are 5 pounds 5 ounces; 6 pounds 7 ounces; 7 pounds 8 ounces; and 5 pounds 15 ounces."

"Do you have any information that might help sort this out?"

"Well, some." The secretary gathered a few of the slips. "Jennifer was born in March. The Sartorius boy was born on April 4. At least two of the babies are heavier than Frederick. The heaviest baby was born two days later than the Shirley baby, and the Wagner girl was born three days before the baby that weighed six pounds and seven ounces."

"Hmmm." Stanwick frowned. "Anything more?"

"Well, I remember that the smallest baby was either the first or the last one born. Oh, and the Lee baby was not eight ounces lighter than the Shirley baby, who is not Frederick."

Stanwick laughed.

"You certainly have an eclectic memory, Louise," he said. "If it's accurate, however, we have enough information to match the names, dates, and weights for the bulletin announcements."

What is the full name, birthdate, and weight of each baby?

Solution on page 93.

Stanwick at the Circus

THE APPEARANCE one summer morning of a large tent in the southeast corner of the Baskerville playground could mean only one thing: the Richard Brothers one-ring circus was back in town.

Early that morning, Thomas P. Stanwick and his Labrador, Rufus, were walking among the stalls, trailers, and piles of equipment and canvas that constitute the impedimenta of even a small circus. The amateur logician admired the almost military precision with which the company of performers and crew set the circus up.

"Good morning, dear sir!" said a voice behind him.

Stanwick turned to see a cheery man with white hair and a florid face, wearing a baggy black suit, an elaborate bow tie, a silk hat, and a vest with a watch chain.

"Professor McFuddle!" exclaimed Stanwick. shaking his hand. "Welcome back. How is everyone at Richard Brothers?"

"Just fine, Thomas," McFuddle replied with a laugh. "Of course, since Wanda the contortionist ran off to join an accounting firm, Mr. Richard has been trying to reorganize the acts. It's had him perplexed, I don't mind telling you."

"Why is that?"

"Well, Delpho the acrobat and Jilko the juggler demand the same amount of time for their acts. (A bit of professional jealousy there.) Carlo the elephant trainer won't go on first, but insists on going on before Delpho. He also needs three times as much time as Delpho.

"Bobo the clown needs only half as much time as Carlo," the professor continued, "but he refuses to be the last of the four to go on. Of the four, Jilko goes on third. There are some other acts, including mine, that take a total of 46 minutes. The whole show lasts two and a half hours."

"And Mr. Richard, I suppose, is trying to accommodate the performers by putting them in the right order," said Stanwick.

"Exactly. He is also trying to make sure he can give them each enough time."

Stanwick whistled to Rufus, who was starting to wander.

"Well, Professor," he said, "if it isn't too early to see Mr. Richard, I think I can point out an order of performance the performers can live with and how much time each will require. The show must go on!"

How much time will each act need, and in what order?

Solution on page 91.

SOLUTIONS

Murder at Big Jake's (page 34)—Since he was identified at the bar, Gummond's first statement is false. Under either variation of the disorder, his second statement is therefore true. The content of that statement implies the truth of the fourth statement as well.

If Gummond were lying every third statement, his fourth statement (three after the false first statement) would be false, which it isn't. Thus he is lying every other statement. Gummond's third statement is therefore false, and he did the shooting.

Memorial Day Mischief (page 46)—Stanwick suspected the young man in the T-shirt. Only he had the sort of footwear (sneakers) that would have been quiet enough on a hardwood floor for him to have committed the crime in absolute silence.

A Model Murder (page 10)—Phillips was the killer.

Walker had told him only that Lola had been found dead in the house. Without being the killer, Phillips would not have known when he entered the house that she had been stabbed upstairs.

Phillips's trial revealed that Lola had broken off with him during their lunch. He had killed her out of jealousy and was convicted of the crime.

The Powers' Predicament (page 64)—Stanwick knew that the family could not repeatedly sleep in the car with the motor running (which would be necessary for the heat to work) without likely being asphyxiated by carbon monoxide. This is the first flaw.

The capitalized words in the letter (indicating the name and town of the recipient) would also change with each letter recipient. Presumably the Powers children would study in the same library each day. The location of the library, however, was in capitals (the second flaw), and would therefore vary with each letter.

A New Year's Dissolution (page 17)—If the poison was not administered by food, drink, or inhalation (since no one else was affected), it must have been administered by touch, through the victim's skin pores.

The only thing Dunhope touched shortly before his collapse that he hadn't touched earlier, and that no one else had touched, was the inside of the napkin served with his hors d'oeuvres. (Remember that Miss Schultze was still holding a napkin.) Therefore this had been doctored with poison.

The critical event was Dunhope's being bumped and spilling his Champagne. Since he was not carrying a handkerchief, he must have opened his napkin to clean up the spill and so touched the poison. Only Henson had helped serve the hors d'oeuvres (and napkins) and then bumped Dunhope, causing him to open his napkin. Henson was therefore the logical suspect.

Walker's investigation bore out Stanwick's conclusions. Henson was convicted of murdering his partner to gain full control of their lucrative agency.

The Bracken Park Incident (page 54)—Stanwick suspected Kramer because the news vendor claimed to recognize the victim when Stanwick mentioned the Harvard sweatshirt. Miss Vaneer had also worn a jacket with a reflector, which of course would have been worn over the sweatshirt. The vendor would therefore not have known what the sweatshirt looked like unless he had been the attacker, who had to open the jacket to get to the moneybelt around her stomach.

Even if Vaneer had worn the sweatshirt on previous jogs, Kramer would by his statement have seen her only during the previous two weeks, when the seasonal chill would still have required her to wear the same layers of clothing.

Death at the Clinic (page 38)—McGowan arrived two and a half hours after Rosella's opened, at 11:30 A.M. He was there half an hour before and after the noon whistle, and so left at 12:30 P.M. Workman arrived 45 minutes later, at 1:15 P.M., and stayed at least half an hour. Since Lola died at 1:44 P.M., he was the killer.

Beard arrived at 2:30 P.M., at the end of an hour-long soap opera that began at 1:30 P.M., found Lola dead, and left.

The Tale of the Generous Rajah (page 76)—Morton Henry Stanley was correct in asserting that, if he could know what was in one chest, all of which were mislabeled, he could deduce what was in the other two. Suppose he had succeeded in opening the middle chest, the one with the emerald sign. It would have contained either diamonds or rubies. If it had contained diamonds, then the rubies would have been in the chest with the diamond sign and the emeralds would have been in the chest with the ruby sign. If it had instead contained rubies, then the diamonds would have been in the chest with the ruby sign and the emeralds would have been in the chest with the diamond sign. Only by these combinations could all three chests have the wrong signs. Had he chosen and opened one of the other two chests, similar reasoning would have revealed the contents of all three.

Unfortunately for the good explorer, he failed to notice that the rajah had said that the befuddled servant had failed in each of his attempts to match a sign to the right chest. As Stanwick noticed, there were in fact four such attempts, the first being when the servant put the emerald sign on the first trunk. Only after that did he arrange the signs in their final order (diamond-emerald-ruby). This meant that the first trunk contained neither emeralds nor diamonds. It therefore contained the rubies. Since the second chest had the emerald sign, the emeralds must have been in the third chest, and the diamonds must have been in the second.

The offer of a lockpick was therefore an unnecessary ruse. Stanwick knew this, but Morton Henry Stanley never suspected it.

The Phony Faith Healer (page 49)— The blind man had supposedly been blind only since the age of 20, and thus was credible in identifying the color purple. Similarly, the deaf man could read lips and speak somewhat, and thus could credibly respond to Howsham's question.

However, when Howsham turned him toward the audience and looked up, the man could no longer read his lips. No man deaf from birth could thus have instantly understood and responded to Howsham's exclamation "Hallelujah! He is healed!" solely by its sound, as the supposedly newly healed man did. He was therefore an accomplice of Howsham's.

One Morning at the Festival (page 60)—If Hagman were a liar, then Leary and Glasker would both be truthtellers. Glasker would also be a liar, because of Leary's second statement. Since this is impossible, Hagman is a truthteller. Parrella therefore never attends the festival, so Glasker is a liar. Since Parrella's first statement is a restatement of Hagman's second statement, Parrella is also a truthteller.

Since Glasker is a liar, by her first statement the thief must be either Hagman or Leary. By Parrella's second statement, however, Hagman is not the thief. The thief is therefore Leary.

When presented with this reasoning, Leary confessed to stealing Miss Porky Pine for culinary reasons. She was returned intact.

Death Brings Down the Curtain (page 24)—Stanwick noticed that the movements of the first "victim," Mort Hooper, were not independently confirmed. His character having been shot, he would not have had to reappear on stage until the curtain call, so no one else cared where he was until then. He was therefore the prime suspect, and was eventually found to have committed the crime out of obsessive jealousy.

The Stockbroker's Last Morning (page 7)—Golding said Steinberg was seized with convulsions as soon as the coffee cup left his lips, and that no one had been in the room since his death. If this were true, the coffee cup would not have been placed back on the saucer, where Stanwick found it.

Golding had actually entered Steinberg's office from his own office while Steinberg was sipping his coffee and reading the paper in the easy chair. Engaging Steinberg in conversation, Golding slipped poison from the vial into the coffee. Steinberg drank it and died. Golding then (erroneously) replaced the cup, refolded the paper, and put it aside. Wiping his prints from the vial, he put Steinberg's prints on it and put it in the dead man's pocket. He then typed the suicide note (wearing gloves), went back into his office through the connecting door, entered the reception area, picked up the newsletter documents, and enacted his version of the tragedy.

Golding eventually confessed to murdering his mentor to advance his own career.

Sabotage at Centipore (page 51)—The records of the storage room terminal establish that the alteration was done on an outside computer, which required the use of a decryption code. Anyone other than the senior engineers would have had to get the new code through Freedman, who was out sick all that week. Therefore one of the senior engineers altered the disk.

If Miller were the culprit, he would have at least delayed his pretended discovery. The competitor thus selected Donlan or Delaney. Selecting Donlan would have been pointless, however, since he would have needed the cooperation of one of the others. He could not enter the storage room alone, and the location of the disk there would have made it very difficult for him to remove it without the engineer with him being aware of it. The selected, and guilty, engineer is therefore Delaney.

The Case of the Bulgonian Spy (page 58)—Perry was away from his papers between 9:00 and 9:15. Gulkovo left the bar at 8:45 and did not return to the bar until 9:15. Impalus, however, returned to the bar at 8:45 and could have remained until as late as 9:15. Only he, therefore, had the opportunity to steal the papers.

Murder by the Wayward (page 36)—Since Lubbock died by his car with his key case in his hand, he was preparing to drive away, probably in pursuit of Thurston. If he had seen her or her parked car, he would have approached her or looked for her instead.

He was shot from the direction of the hedge. She could therefore have shot him only by moving her car out of sight and then returning to hide and wait for him. He left the inn so soon after she did, however, that there was not enough time for that. She therefore did not shoot him.

An Idyll Day in Edinburgh (page 66)—The customer said he had bought the book for a lower price at another shop. If this were so, however, he would not have known what the present shop owner charged for the book, since there were no other copies in the shop. He would only have known the shop owner's price by seeing it in the book in the present shop before erasing it.

Stanwick at the Circus (page 84)—The whole show takes 150 minutes, and the other acts take 46 minutes, so these four acts take 104 minutes. This equals Carlo's time plus half of Carlo's time (for Bobo) plus one-third of Carlo's time (for Delpho) plus another third of Carlo's time (for Jilko, whose time equals that of Delpho). The 104 minutes therefore equals thirteen-sixths of Carlo's time, so Carlo's time is 48 minutes. Bobo's time is therefore 24 minutes, and Delpho and Jilko each need 16 minutes.

Jilko is third. Carlo is not first, last, or third, so he is second. Delpho follows Carlo, and so must be fourth. Bobo by elimination is first.

The Case of the Invisible Murderer (page 20)—The circumstances of Hottleman's death make suicide or natural death impossible, so he was murdered. The murderer must have entered the room through the main doorway after Hottleman re-entered it following his return of the sunglasses.

Stanwick's main clue was the condition of the tables in the murder room. Only the victim's table still had dirty utensils and dishes. The others, including whichever table the elderly couple had used, had been cleared. Nothing had been touched after the discovery of the body, so the tables must have been cleared before then but after the couple had left. Only one person could have done this without seeming out of place or attracting even the slightest notice from the preoccupied owner: the "invisible" busboy. The busboy was therefore the murderer.

Subsequent investigation by Walker proved that Stanwick's deduction was correct. The busboy had murdered the wealthy Hottleman for his wallet.

A Death by the Thames (page 30)—The maid mentioned the missing silver and jewels. She could have seen the rifled silver case, which was in the living room, but could not have known about the jewels missing from the bedroom if, as she claimed, she had only been in the living room before fleeing the flat.

Miss Woolbrott eventually confessed that she had helped her boyfriend ransack the flat, and that he had killed Sir Alan when the industrialist returned home unexpectedly early.

The Case of the Royston Reindeer (page 43)—Coughlin's office was west of the harbor, so he was looking into the harbor on a clear day, facing the newly rising sun. Though he would have been able to see the swimmers and probably even any boats, the glare and shadows would have made impossible his reading the names of the boats from a distance.

Stanwick at Chartwell (page 74)—The bachelor historian from Oldham was one of the two men, but not Martin (who hated to write), and thus was Colville.

Pearman was not from Woodford, Epping (Martin), or Oldham (Colville), and so was from Dundee. She therefore was not the painter, the bricklayer, or the historian (Colville), and so was the novelist.

Thompson, who must by elimination have come from Woodford, could not have laid bricks without a trowel, so she must have been the painter, leaving Martin, as the bricklayer.

In summary: Thompson was the painter from Woodford; Martin was the bricklayer from Epping; Colville was the historian from Oldham; and Pearman was the novelist from Dundee.

Chief Ryan Pays a Call (page 62)—Leader, who has the highest rank, is not Wynant, who is outranked, or Bobbin (given), or Aronisi (Driver), and therefore is Janison. Weapons is not Wynant (given), or Janison (Leader), or Aronisi (Driver), and therefore is Bobbin. Wynant by elimination is Muscle.

Leader has the highest rank, so Weapons, just below Leader, is second. Driver does not have the lowest rank, and thus is third. Muscle therefore is fourth.

The Prom Date Puzzle (page 70)—Marlene is the tallest of them all, so she must go with George, the only boy who doesn't mind a taller date. Harvey can't go with Deb, who is taller. Nor can he go with Lizbeth, who had a lower grade point average. Harvey must therefore go with Annette.

This leaves Roger and Brian to pair up with Lizbeth and Deb. Since Deb won't slow-dance, she can't go with Roger, so she must go with Brian, and Roger must go with Lizbeth.

Death of a Kingpin (page 27)—Griffith's dying message indicates that his killer was one of the "Rens." The guard was attacked at close range with little or no warning. His lack of alertness indicates that the visitors had already left, so the killer must have returned. Had the killer approached from the end of the long hardwood hallway, he would have been seen or heard first. He must therefore have used the secret passage and suddenly opened the panel and sprung out to attack the guard (and then Griffith).

Only one of the "Rens" would likely have known of the existence of the secret passage: Griffith's former personal assistant, Rennecker. Stanwick therefore deduced (correctly, as Walker's investigation found) that Rennecker was the killer.

Babies for the Bulletin (page 82)—Since there is only one two-day gap in the dates, the Shirley baby was born on April 2, and the seven-pound, eight-ounce baby was born on April 4 and is therefore the Sartorius boy. The smallest (five pounds, five ounces) baby was not born on April 4, so he or she was born on March 27. The Sartorius boy is not Frederick (who is not the heaviest baby) and is therefore Wolfgang.

The Shirley baby is not Jennifer (born in March) or Frederick (given) or Wolfgang (born April 4), and so is Lucile. The Wagner girl is therefore Jennifer. Frederick is therefore the Lee baby. Frederick is one of the two smallest babies (given), but does not weigh five pounds, fifteen ounces (since then Lucile Shirley, who has a different birthday from the smallest baby, would be the six-pound, seven-ounce baby and would thus be eight ounces heavier than Frederick Lee, which is contrary to what is given). Frederick is therefore the smallest baby, at five pounds, five ounces, and so was born on March 27. Jennifer by elimination was born on March 30.

The six-pound, seven-ounce baby was therefore born on April 2 (three days after the Wagner baby, as given), and is therefore Lucile Shirley. The five-pound, fifteen-ounce baby is therefore Jennifer.

In summary: Frederick Lee, 5 lb. 5 oz., was born on March 27. Jennifer Wagner, 5 lbs. 15 oz., was born on March 30. Lucile Shirley, 6 lbs. 7oz., was born on April 2. Wolfgang Sartorius, 7 lbs. 8 oz., was born on April 4.

The Adventure of the Negative Clue (page 13)—If Orrison had just finished slicing fish all morning, he would have retained a noticeable odor of fish, especially on a warm day. While Walker was questioning him, however, the shop had only a metallic odor. The absence of a sharp fish odor was the negative clue.

The Table of Death (page 32)—Stanwick deduced that a man planning to take part in a suicide would not bother to fold and put away a gasoline receipt, but that a salesman expecting to live and write the expense off his income taxes would.

Barnes secretly poisoned Hunter during a cult ritual, and then prepared the "suicide" note and poisoned himself.

Room at the Inn (page 68)—If the first villager is telling the truth, then the second villager is lying, and if the first villager is lying, then the second villager is telling the truth.

Now suppose the third villager is lying. Then the first clause of his statement would be true (since he and one of the other two would be liars). His disjunctive statement as a whole would then be true, which is impossible for a liar. Therefore the third villager is telling the truth. His first clause is therefore false (since only one of the three can be lying), so for his statement as a whole to be true, his second clause must be true.

Therefore the first and third villagers are telling the truth, the second villager is lying, and there is room at the inn.

The Case of the Bulgarian Diamonds (page 56)—If Thorpe's first statement (T1) is true, then both of Lambert's statements (L1 and L2) are false. This contradicts the premise that each made one true and one false statement, so T1 is false and T2 is true. Therefore neither Sorenson nor Cameron was the bookkeeper, and Sorensen was not the printer. Since she was not the salesman either (the salesman having been one of the men), she must have been the banker. This means that C1 is true, so C2 is false and Cameron was not the printer. He must therefore be the salesman.

This proves that S2 if false, so S1 is true and Lambert was not the printer. Lambert was therefore the bookkeeper, and Thorpe was the printer.

The Stolen War Club Caper (page 40)—Raposa belongs to Alpha Gamma Quad. Vokanian claims to have been bar-hopping, so he is not the Flag & Feathers member, who claims to have been in the library. He therefore belongs to the Mausoleum, and Walton belongs to the Flag & Feathers.

Walton is the history major. Raposa is not the geography major, so Vokanian must be the geography major, and Raposa must be the engineering major.

Vokanian claims to have been bar-hopping on the night of the theft. The Flag & Feathers member (Walton) claims to have been studying in the library. Raposa is therefore the one with the alibi of working in the computer center.

The thief is not the person with the computer-center alibi (Raposa) or the Flag & Feathers member (Walton). Therefore the thief is Vokanian.

The Case of the Contentious Cows (page 80)—To meet the conditions of the problem, Stanwick suggested the following sequence: 1) Take a black cow across. 2) Take a black cow and a brown cow across, and bring a black cow back. 3) Take two brown cows across. 4) Take two black cows across. 5) Take the last black cow across.

Stanwick Solves a Pie Puzzle (page 72)—At least one of the remaining pies was baked by Gertie, who had sold only one or two. She had had one pie in the front row and two in the middle row, so the blueberry pie in the back row could not have been hers. She had therefore baked the cherry pie in the center.

The blueberry pie in the back was not baked by Gertie or by Hazel, who had sold hers. It was therefore baked by Frieda.

Index

(Answer pages are in italic type.)

Adventure of the Negative Clue, The, 13, *94*

Babies for the Bulletin, 82, *93*

Bracken Park Incident, The, 54, *87*

Case of the Bulgarian Diamonds, The, 56, *94*

Case of the Bulgonian Spy, The, 58, *90*

Case of the Contentious Cows, The, 80, *95*

Case of the Invisible Murderer, The, 20, *91*

Case of the Royston Reindeer, The, 43, *92*

Chief Ryan Pays a Call, 62, *92*

Death at the Clinic, 38, *87*

Death Brings Down the Curtain, 24, *89*

Death by the Thames, A, 30, *91*

Death of a Kingpin, 27, *93*

Idyll Day in Edinburgh, An, 66, *90*

Introduction, 5

Memorial Day Mischief, 46, *86*

Model Murder, A, 10, *86*

Murder at Big Jake's, 34, *86*

Murder by the Wayward, 36, *90*

New Year's Dissolution, A, 17, *87*

One Morning at the Festival, 60, *89*

Phony Faith Healer, The, 49, *88*

Powers' Predicament, The, 64, *86*

Prom Date Puzzle, The, 70, *92*

Room at the Inn, 68, *94*

Sabotage at Centipore, 51, *90*

Stanwick at Chartwell, 74, *92*

Stanwick at the Circus, 84, *91*

Stanwick Solves a Pie Puzzle, 72, *95*

Stockbroker's Last Morning, The, 7, *89*

Stolen War Club Caper, The, 40, *95*

Table of Death, The, 32, *94*

Tale of the Generous Rajah, The, 76, *88*